C-700
ISBN 0-8373-0700-7

THE PASSBOOK® SERIES

PASSBOOKS®

FOR

CAREER OPPORTUNITIES

SANITATION MAN

National Learning Corporation

212 Michael Drive, Syosset, New York 11791

(516) 921-8888

Copyright © 1990 by

National Learning Corporation

212 Michael Drive, Syosset, New York 11791
(516) 921-8888

PRINTED IN THE UNITED STATES OF AMERICA

PASSBOOK SERIES®

The *PASSBOOK SERIES*® has been created to prepare applicants and candidates for the ultimate academic battlefield — the examination room.

At some time in our lives, each and every one of us may be required to take an examination — for validation, matriculation, admission, qualification, registration, certification, or licensure.

Based on the assumption that every applicant or candidate has met the basic formal educational standards, has taken the required number of courses, and read the necessary texts, the *PASSBOOK SERIES*® furnishes the one special preparation which may assure passing with confidence, instead of failing with insecurity. Examination questions — together with answers — are furnished as the basic vehicle for study so that the mysteries of the examination and its compounding difficulties may be eliminated or diminished by a sure method.

This book is meant to help you pass your examination provided that you qualify and are serious in your objective.

The entire field is reviewed through the huge store of content information which is succinctly presented through a provocative and challenging approach — the question-and-answer method.

A climate of success is established by furnishing the correct answers at the end of each test.

You soon learn to recognize types of questions, forms of questions, and patterns of questioning. You may even begin to anticipate expected outcomes.

You perceive that many questions are repeated or adapted so that you gain acute insights, which may enable you to score many sure points.

You learn how to confront new questions, or types of questions, and to attack them confidently and work out the correct answers.

You note objectives and emphases, and recognize pitfalls and dangers, so that you may make positive educational adjustments.

Moreover, you are kept fully informed in relation to new concepts, methods, practices, and directions in the field.

You discover that you are actually taking the examination all the time: you are preparing for the examination by "taking" an examination, not by reading extraneous and/or supererogatory textbooks.

In short, this PASSBOOK,® used directedly, should be an important factor in helping you to pass your test.

SANITATION MAN

DUTIES AND RESPONSIBILITIES
  Under direct supervision, performs the work and operates the
equipment involved in street cleaning, waste collection, snow removal, and waste disposal; performs related work.

EXAMPLES OF TYPICAL TASKS
  Operates all types of motorized equipment used in connection with
street cleaning, waste collection, snow removal and waste disposal
operations. Manually cleans streets; loads and unloads waste materials; removes waste from dumping boards; moors and shifts barges;
disinfects and covers barges.

TESTS
  The written test will be designed to measure ability to understand
written material, to fill out forms, to understand traffic signs and
symbols, and to do basic arithmetic.

MEDICAL STANDARDS
  Eligibles will be required to pass a qualifying medicial test to
prior to appointment. Candidates will be required to meet the medi-
cal and physical standards which have been established.

HOW TO TAKE A TEST

I. YOU MUST PASS AN EXAMINATION

A. *WHAT EVERY CANDIDATE SHOULD KNOW*

Examination applicants often ask us for help in preparing for the written test. What can I study in advance? What kinds of questions will be asked? How will the test be given? How will the papers be graded?

As an applicant for a civil service examination, you may be wondering about some of these things. Our purpose here is to suggest effective methods of advance study and to describe civil service examinations.

Your chances for success on this examination can be increased if you know how to prepare. Those "pre-examination jitters" can be reduced if you know what to expect. You can even experience an adventure in good citizenship if you know why civil service examinations are given.

B. *WHY ARE CIVIL SERVICE EXAMINATIONS GIVEN?*

Civil service examinations are important to you in two ways. As a citizen, you want public jobs filled by employees who know how to do their work. As a job-seeker, you want a fair chance to compete for that job on an equal footing with other candidates. The best known means of accomplishing this two-fold goal is the competitive examination.

Examinations are widely publicized throughout the nation. They may be administered for jobs in federal, state, city, municipal, town, or village governments or agencies.

Any citizen may apply, with some limitations, such as the age or residence of applicants. Your experience and education may be reviewed to see whether you meet the requirements for the particular examination. When these requirements exist, they are reasonable and are applied consistently to all applicants. Thus, a competitive examination may cause you some uneasiness now, but it is your privilege and safeguard.

C. *HOW ARE CIVIL SERVICE EXAMINATIONS DEVELOPED?*

Examinations are carefully written by trained technicians who are specialists in the field known as "psychological measurement," in consultation with recognized authorities in the field of work that the test will cover. These experts recommend the subject matter areas or skills to be tested; only those knowledges or skills important to your success on the job are included. The most reliable books and source materials available are used as references. Together, the experts and technicians judge the difficulty level of the questions.

Test technicians know how to phrase questions so that the problem is clearly stated. Their ethics do not permit "trick" or "catch" questions. Questions may have been tried out on sample groups, or subjected to statistical analysis, to determine their usefulness.

Written tests are often used in combination with performance tests, ratings of training and experience, and oral interviews. All of these measures combine to form the best known means of finding the right man for the right job.

II. HOW TO PASS THE WRITTEN TEST

A. *NATURE OF THE EXAMINATION*

To prepare intelligently for civil service examinations, you should know how they differ from school examinations you have taken. In school you were assigned certain definite pages to read or subjects to cover. The examination questions were quite detailed and usually emphasized memory. Civil service examinations, on the other hand, try to discover your present ability to perform the duties of a position, plus your potentiality to learn these duties. In other words, a civil service examination attempts to predict how successful you will be. Questions cover such a broad area that they cannot be as minute and detailed as school examination questions.

In the public service similar kinds of work, or positions, are grouped together in one "class." This process is known as "position-classification." All the positions in a class are paid according to the salary range for that class. One class title covers all these positions, and they are all tested by the same examination.

B. *FOUR BASIC STEPS*

1. Study the Announcement.--How, then, can you know what subjects to study? Our best answer is: "Learn as much as possible about the class of positions for which you have applied." The examination will test the knowledge, skills, and abilities needed to do the work.

Your most valuable source of information about the position you want is the official announcement of the examination. This announcement lists the training and experience qualifications. Check these standards and apply only if you come reasonably close to meeting them.

The brief description of the position in the examination announcement offers some clues to the subjects which will be tested. Think about the job itself. Review the duties in your mind. Can you perform them, or are there some in which you are rusty? Fill in the blank spots in your preparation.

Many jurisdictions preview the written test in the examination announcement by including a section called "Knowledge and Abilities Required," "Scope of Examination," or some similar heading. Here you will find out specifically what fields will be tested.

2. Review Your Own Background.-- Once you learn in general what the position is all about, and what you need to know to do the work, ask yourself which subjects you already know fairly well and which need improvement. You may wonder whether to concentrate on improving your strong areas or on building some background in your fields of weakness. When the announcement has specified "some knowledge" or "considerable knowledge," or has used adjectives such as "beginning principles of ...." or "advanced .....methods," you can get a clue as to the number and difficulty of questions to be asked in any given field. More questions, and hence broader coverage, would be included for those subjects which are more important in the work. Now weigh your strengths and weaknesses against the job requirements and prepare accordingly.

3. Determine the Level of the Position.-- Another way to tell how intensively you should prepare is to understand the level of the job for which you are applying. Is it the entering level? In other words, is this the position in which beginners in a field of work are hired? Or is it an intermediate or advanced level? Sometimes this is indicated by such words as "Junior" or "Senior" in the class title.Other jurisdictions use Roman numerals to designate the level: Clerk I,

Clerk II, for example. The word "Supervisor" sometimes appears in the title. If the level is not indicated by the title, check the description of duties. Will you be working under very close supervision, or will you have responsibility for independent decisions in this work?

4. Choose Appropriate Study Materials.-- Now that you know the subjects to be examined and the relative amount of each subject to be covered, you can choose suitable study materials. For beginning level jobs, or even advanced ones, if you have a pronounced weakness in some aspect of your training, read a modern, standard textbook in that field. Be sure it is up-to-date and has general coverage. Such books are normally available at your library, and the librarian will be glad to help you locate one. For entry level positions, questions of appropriate difficulty are chosen -- neither highly advanced questions, nor those too simple. Such questions require careful thought but not advanced training.

If the position for which you are applying is technical or advanced, you will read more advanced, specialized material. If you are already familiar with the basic principles of your field, elementary textbooks would waste your time. Concentrate on advanced textbooks and technical periodicals. Think through the concepts and review difficult problems in your field.

These are all general sources. You can get more ideas on your own initiative, following these leads. For example, training manuals and publications of the government agency which employs workers in your field can be useful, particularly for technical and professional positions. A letter or visit to the government department involved may result in more specific study suggestions, and certainly will provide you with a more definite idea of the exact nature of the position you are seeking.

III. KINDS OF TESTS

Tests are used for purposes other than measuring knowledge and ability to perform specified duties. For some positions, it is equally important to test ability to make adjustments to new situations or to profit from training. In others, basic mental abilities not dependent upon information are essential. Questions which test these things may not appear as pertinent to the duties of the position as those which test for knowledge and information. Yet they are often highly important parts of a fair examination. For very general questions, it is almost impossible to help you direct your study efforts. What we can do is to point out some of the more common of these general abilities needed in public service positions and describe some typical questions.

1. General Information

Broad, general information has been found useful for predicting job success in some kinds of work. This is tested in a variety of ways, from vocabulary lists to questions about current events. Basic background in some field of work, such as sociology or economics, may be sampled in a group of questions. Often these are principles which have become familiar to most persons through "exposure" rather than through formal training. It is difficult to advise you how to study for these questions; being alert to the world around you is our best suggestion.

2. Verbal Ability

An example of an ability needed in many positions is verbal or language ability. Verbal ability is, in brief, the ability to use and understand words. Vocabulary and grammar tests are typical measures of this ability. "Reading comprehension" or "paragraph interpretation" questions are common in many kinds of civil service tests. You are given a paragraph of written material and asked to find its central meaning.

3. Numerical Ability

Number skills can be tested by the familiar arithmetic problem, by checking paired lists of numbers to see which are alike and which are different, or by interpreting charts and graphs. In the latter test, a graph may be printed in the test booklet which you are asked to use as the basis for answering questions.

4. Observation

A popular test for law-enforcement positions is the observation test. A picture is shown to you for several minutes, then taken away. Questions about the picture test your ability to observe both details and larger elements.

5. Following Directions

In many positions in the public service, the employee must be able to carry out written instructions dependably and accurately. You may be given a chart with several columns, each column listing a variety of information. The questions require you to carry out directions involving the information given in the chart.

6. Skills and Aptitudes

Performance tests effectively measure some manual skills and aptitudes. When the skill is one in which you are trained, such as typing or shorthand, you can practice. These tests are often very much like those given in business school or high school courses. For many of the other skills and aptitudes, however, no short-time preparation can be made. Skills and abilities natural to you or that you have developed throughout your lifetime are being tested.

Many of the general questions just described provide all the data needed to answer the questions and ask you to use your reasoning ability to find the answers. Your best preparation for these tests, as well as for tests of facts and ideas, is to be at your physical and mental best. You, no doubt, have your own methods of getting into an exam-taking mood and keeping "in shape." The next section lists some ideas on this subject.

IV. KINDS OF QUESTIONS

Only rarely is the "essay" question, which you answer in narrative form, used in civil service tests. Civil service tests are usually of the short-answer type. Full instructions for answering these questions will be given to you at the examination. But in case this is your first experience with short-answer questions and separate answer sheets, here is what you need to know.

1. Multiple-Choice Questions

Most popular of the short-answer questions is the "multiple-choice" or "best-answer" question. It can be used, for example, to test for factual knowledge, ability to solve problems, or judgment in meeting situations found at work.

A multiple-choice question is normally one of three types:

(1) It can begin with an incomplete statement followed by several possible endings. You are to find the one ending which *best* completes the statement, although some of the others may not be entirely wrong.

(2) It can also be a complete statement in the form of a question which is answered by choosing one of the statements listed.

(3) It can be in the form of a problem -- again you select the best answer.

Here is an example of a multiple-choice question with a discussion which should give you some clues as to the method for choosing the right answer.

SAMPLE QUESTION:

When an employee has a complaint about his assignment, the action which will *best* help him overcome his difficulty is

    (A) to discuss his difficulty with his co-workers
    (B) to take the problem to the head of the organization
    (C) to take the problem to the person who gave him the assignment
    (D) to say nothing to anyone about his complaint

In answering this question you should study each of the choices to find which is best. Consider choice (A). Certainly an employee may discuss his complaint with fellow employees, but no change or improvement can result, and the complaint remains unsolved. Choice (B) is a poor choice since the head of the organization probably does not know what assignment you have been given, and taking your problem to him is known as "going over the head" of the supervisor. The supervisor, or person who made the assignment, is the person who can clarify it or correct any injustice. Choice (C) is, therefore, correct. To say nothing, as in choice (D), is unwise. Supervisors have an interest in knowing the problems employees are facing, and the employee is seeking a solution to his problem.

2. True-False Questions

The "true-false" or "right-wrong" form of question is sometimes used. Here a complete statement is given. Your problem is to decide whether the statement is right or wrong.

SAMPLE QUESTION:

A person-to-person long distance telephone call costs less than a station-to-station call to the same city.

This question is wrong, or "false," since person-to-person calls are more expensive.

This is not a complete list of all possible question forms, although most of the others are variations of these common types. You will always get complete directions for answering questions. Be sure you understand *how* to mark your answers -- ask questions until you do.

V. RECORDING YOUR ANSWERS

For an examination with very few applicants, you may be told to record your answers in the test booklet itself. Separate answer sheets are much more common. If this separate answer sheet is to be scored by machine -- and this is often the case -- it is highly important that you mark your answers correctly in order to get credit.

An electric test-scoring machine is often used in civil service offices because of the speed with which papers can be scored. Machine-scored answer sheets must be marked with a special pencil, which will be given to you. This pencil has a high graphite content which responds to the electrical scoring machine. As a matter of fact, stray dots may register as answers, so do not let your pencil rest on the answer sheet while you are pondering the correct answer. Also, if your pencil lead breaks or is otherwise defective, ask for another.

Since the answer sheet will be dropped in a slot in the scoring machine, be careful not to bend the corners or get the paper crumpled.

The answer sheet normally has five vertical columns of numbers, with 30 numbers to a column. These numbers correspond to the question numbers in your test booklet. After each number, going across the page, are four or five pairs of dotted lines. These short dotted lines have small letters or numbers above them. The first two pairs may also have a "T" and "F" above the letters. This indicates that the first two pairs only are to be used if the questions are of the true-false type. If the questions are multiple-choice, disregard this "T" and "F" completely, and pay attention only to the small number or letters.

Answer your questions in the manner of the sample that follows. Proceed in the sequential steps outlined below.

Assume that you are answering question 32, which is:

    32. The largest city in the United States is:
        A. Washington, D.C.   B. New York City   C. Chicago
        D. Detroit   E. San Francisco

1. Choose the answer you think is best.
    New York City is the largest, so choice B is correct.
2. Find the row of dotted lines numbered the same as the question you are answering.
    This is question number 32, so find row number 32.
3. Find the pair of dotted lines corresponding to the answer you have chosen.
    You have chosen answer B, so find the pair of dotted lines marked "B".
4. Make a solid black mark between the dotted lines.
    Go up and down two or three times with your pencil so plenty of graphite rubs off, but do not let the mark get outside or above the dots.

VI. BEFORE THE TEST

Common sense will help you find procedures to follow to get ready for an examination. Too many of us, however, overlook these sensible measures. Indeed, nervousness and fatigue have been found to be the most serious reasons why applicants fail to do their best on civil service tests. Here is a list of reminders.

1. Begin Your Preparation Early

Don't wait until the last minute to go scurrying around for books and materials or to find out what the position is all about.

2. Prepare Continuously

An hour a night for a week is better than an all-night cram session. This has been definitely established. What is more, a night a week for a month will return better dividends than crowding your study into a shorter period of time.

3. Locate the Place of the Examination

You have been sent a notice telling you when and where to report for the examination. If the location is in a different town or otherwise unfamiliar to you, it would be well to inquire the best route and learn something about the building.

4. Relax the Night Before the Test

Allow your mind to rest. Do not study at all that night. Plan some mild recreation or diversion; then go to bed early and get a good night's sleep.

5. Get Up Early Enough to Make a Leisurely Trip to the Place for the Test

Then unforeseen events, traffic snarls, unfamiliar buildings, will not upset you.

6. Dress Comfortably

A written test is not a fashion show. You will be known by number and not by name, so wear something comfortable.

7. Leave Excess Paraphernalia at Home

Shopping bags and odd bundles will get in your way. You need bring only the items mentioned in the official notice sent to you; usually everything you need is provided. Do not bring reference books to the examination. They will only confuse those last minutes and be taken away from you when in the test room.

8. Arrive Somewhat Ahead of Time

If because of transportation schedules you must get there very early, bring a newspaper or magazine to take your mind off yourself while waiting.

9. Locate the Examination Room

When you have found the proper room, you will be directed to the seat or part of the room where you will sit. Sometimes you are given a sheet of instructions to read while you are waiting. Do not fill out any forms until you are told to do so; just read them and be ready.

10. Relax and Prepare to Listen to the Instructions

11. If you **have any physical problem** that may keep you from doing your best, **be** sure to tell the test administrator. If you are sick, or in poor health, **you really cannot** do your best on the test. You can come back and take the test some other time.

VII. AT THE TEST

The day of the test is here and you have the test booklet in your hand. The temptation to get going is very strong. Caution! There is more to success than knowing the right answers. You must know how to identify your **papers and under**stand variations in the type of short-answer **question used in this** particular examination. Follow these suggestions for maximum results from your efforts:

1. Cooperate with the Monitor

The test administrator has a duty to create a situation in which you can be as much at ease as possible. He will give instructions, tell you when to begin, check to see that you are marking your answer sheet correctly. He is not there to guard you, although he will see that your competitors do not take unfair advantage. He wants to help you do your best.

2. Listen to All Instructions

Don't jump the gun! Wait until you understand all directions. In most civil service tests you get more time than you need to answer the questions. So don't get in a hurry. Read each word of instructions until you clearly understand the meaning. Study the examples. Listen to all announcements. Follow directions. Ask questions if you do not understand what to do.

3. Identify Your Papers

Civil service examinations are usually identified by number only. You will be assigned a number; you must not put your name on your test papers. Be sure to copy your number correctly. Since more than one examination may be given, copy your exact examination title.

4. Plan Your Time

Unless you are told that a test is a "speed" or "rate-of-work" test, speed itself is not usually important. Time enough to answer all the questions will be provided. But this does not mean that you have all day. An overall time limit has been set. Divide the total time (in minutes) by the number of questions to get the approximate time you have for each question.

5. Do Not Linger Over Difficult Questions

If you come across a difficult question, mark it with a paper clip (useful to have along) and come back to it when you have been through the booklet. One caution if you do this -- be sure to skip a number on your answer sheet too. Check often to be sure that you have not lost your place and that you are marking in the row numbered the same as the question you are answering.

6. Read the Questions

Be sure you know what the question asks! Many capable people are unsuccessful because they failed to *read* the questions correctly.

7. Answer All Questions

Unless you have been instructed that a penalty will be deducted for incorrect answers, it is better to guess than to omit a question.

8. Speed Tests

It is often better *not* to guess on speed tests. It has been found that on timed tests people are tempted to spend the last few seconds before time is called in marking answers at random -- without even reading them -- in the hope of picking up a few extra points. To discourage this practice, the instructions may warn you that your score will be "corrected" for guessing. That is, a penalty will be applied. The incorrect answers will be deducted from the correct ones, or some other penalty formula will be used.

9. Review Your Answers

If you finish before time is called, go back to the questions you guessed or omitted to give further thought to them. Review other answers if you have time.

10. **Return Your Test Materials**

If you are ready to leave before others have finished or time is called, take *all* your materials to the monitor and leave quietly. Never take any test material with you. The monitor can discover whose papers are not complete, and taking a test booklet may be grounds for disqualification.

VIII. EXAMINATION TECHNIQUES

1. Read the *general* instructions carefully. These are usually printed on the first page of the examination booklet. As a rule, these instructions refer to the timing of the examination; the fact that you should not start work until the signal and must stop work at a signal, etc. If there are any *special* instructions, such as a choice of questions to be answered, make sure that you note this instruction carefully.

2. When you are ready to start work on the examination, that is as soon as the signal has been given, read the instructions to each question booklet, underline any key words or phrases, such as *least, best, outline, describe,* and the like. In this way you will tend to answer as requested rather than discover on reviewing your paper that you *listed without describing,* that you selected the *worst* choice rather than the *best* choice, etc.

3. If the examination is of the objective or so-called multiple-choice type, that is, each question will also give a series of possible answers: A, B, C, or D, and you are called upon to select the best answer and write the letter next to that answer on your answer paper, it is advisable to start answering each question in turn. There may be anywhere from 50 to 100 such questions in the three or four hours allotted and you can see how much time would be taken if you read through all the questions before beginning to answer any. Furthermore, if you come across a question or a group of questions which you know would be difficult to answer, it would undoubtedly affect your handling of all the other questions.

4. If the examination is of the esssay-type and contains but a few questions, it is a moot point as to whether you should read all the questions before starting to answer any one. Of course if you are given a choice, say five out of seven and the like, then it is essential to read all the questions so you can eliminate the two which are most difficult. If, however, you are asked to answer all the questions, there may be danger in trying to answer the easiest one first because you may find that you will spend too much time on it. The best technique is to answer the first question, then proceed to the second, etc.

5. Time your answers. Before the examination begins, write down the time it started, then add the time allowed for the examination and write down the time it must be completed, then divide the time available somewhat as follows:

(a) If $3\frac{1}{2}$ hours are allowed, that would be 210 minutes. If you have 80 objective-type questions, that would be an average of $2\frac{1}{2}$ minutes per question. Allow yourself no more than 2 minutes per question, or a total of 160 minutes, which will permit about 50 minutes to review.

(b) If for the time allotment of 210 minutes, there are 7 essay questions to answer, that would average about 30 minutes a question. Give yourself only 25 minutes per question so that you have about 35 minutes to review.

6. The most important instruction is *to read each question* and make sure you know what is wanted. The second most important instruction is to *time yourself properly* so that you answer every question. The third most important instruction is to *answer every question.* Guess if you have to but include something for each question. Remember that you will receive no credit for a blank and will probably receive some credit if you write something in answer to an essay question. If you guess a letter, say "B" for a multiple-choice question, you may have guessed right. If you leave a blank as the answer to a multiple-choice question, the examiners may respect your feelings but it will not add a point to your score.

7. Suggestions

    a. <u>Objective-Type Questions</u>

      (1) Examine the question booklet for proper sequence of pages and questions.

      (2) Read all instructions carefully.

      (3) Skip any question which seems too difficult; return to it after all other questions have been answered.

      (4) Apportion your time properly; do not spend too much time on any single question or group of questions.

      (5) Note and underline key words -- *all, most, fewest, least, best, worst, same, opposite.*

      (6) Pay particular attention to negatives.

      (7) Note unusual option, e.g., unduly long, short, complex, different or similar in content to the body of the question.

      (8) Observe the use of "hedging" words -- *probably, may, most likely, etc.*

      (9) Make sure that your answer is put next to the same number as the question.

    (10) Do not second-guess unless you have good reason to believe the second answer is definitely more correct.

    (11) Cross out original answer if you decide another answer is more accurate; do not erase.

    (12) Answer all questions; guess unless instructed otherwise.

    (13) Leave time for review.

    b. <u>Essay-Type Questions</u>

      (1) Read each question carefully.

      (2) Determine exactly what is wanted. Underline key words or phrases.

      (3) Decide on outline or paragraph answer.

      (4) Include many different points and elements unless asked to develop any one or two points or elements.

      (5) Show impartiality by giving pros and cons unless directed to select one side only.

      (6) Make and write down any assumptions you find necessary to answer the question.

      (7) Watch your English, grammar, punctuation, choice of words.

      (8) Time your answers; don't crowd material.

8. Answering the Essay Question

    Most essay questions can be answered by framing the specific response around several key words or ideas. Here are a few such key words or ideas:

M's: manpower, materials, methods, money, management;
P's: purpose, program, policy, plan, procedure, practice, problems, pitfalls, personnel, public relations.

a. Six Basic Steps in Handling Problems:
   (1) Preliminary plan and background development
   (2) Collect information, data and facts
   (3) Analyze and interpret information, data and facts
   (4) Analyze and develop solutions as well as make recommendations
   (5) Prepare report and sell recommendations
   (6) Install recommendations and follow up effectiveness

b. Pitfalls to Avoid
   (1) *Taking things for granted*
       A statement of the situation does not necessarily imply that each of the elements is necessarily true; for example, a complaint may be invalid and biased so that all that can be taken for granted is that a complaint has been registered.
   (2) *Considering only one side of a situation*
       Wherever possible, indicate several alternatives and then point out the reasons you selected the best one.
   (3) *Failing to indicate follow-up*
       Whenever your answer indicates action on your part, make certain that you will take proper follow-up action to see how successful your recommendations, procedures, or actions turn out to be.
   (4) *Taking too long in answering any single question*
       Remember to time your answers properly.

IX. AFTER THE TEST

Scoring procedures differ in detail among civil service jurisdictions although the general principles are the same. Whether the papers are hand-scored or graded by the electric scoring machine we have described, they are nearly always graded by number. That is, the person who marks the paper knows only the number -- never the name -- of the applicant. Not until all the papers have been graded will they be matched with names. If other tests, such as training and experience or oral interview ratings have been given, scores will be combined. Different parts of the examination usually have different weights. For example, the written test might count 60 percent of the final grade, and a rating of training and experience 40 percent. In many jurisdictions, veterans will have a certain number of points added to their grades.

After the final grade has been determined, the names are placed in grade order and an eligible list is established. There are various methods for resolving ties between those who get the same final grade: probably the most common is to place first the name of the person whose application was received first. Job offers are made from the eligible list in the order the names appear on it.

You will be notified of your grade and your rank order as soon as all these computations have been made. This will be done as rapidly as possible.

People who are found to meet the requirements in the announcement are called "eligibles." Their names are put on a list of eligibles. An eligible's chances of getting a job depend on how high he stands on this list and how fast agencies are filling jobs from the list.

When a job is to be filled from a list of eligibles, the agency asks for the names of people on the list of eligibles for that job.

When the civil service commission receives this request, it sends to the agency the names of the three people highest on the list. Or, if the job to be filled has specialized requirements, the office sends the agency, from the general list, the names of the top three persons who meet those requirements.

The appointing officer makes a choice from among the three people whose names were sent to him. If the selected person accepts the appointment, the names of the others are put back on the list to be considered for future openings.

That is the rule in hiring from all kinds of eligible lists, whether they are for typist, carpenter, chemist, or something else. For every vacancy, the appointing officer has his choice of any one of the top three eligibles on the list. This explains why the person whose name is on top of the list sometimes does not get an appointment when some of the persons lower on the list do. If the appointing officer chooses the No.2 or No.3 eligible, the No.1 eligible does not get a job at once, but stays on the list until he is appointed or the list is terminated.

X. HOW TO PASS THE INTERVIEW TEST

The examination for which you applied requires an oral interview test. You have already taken the written test and you are now being called for the interview test -- the final part of the formal examination.

You may think that it is not possible to prepare for an interview test and that there are no procedures to follow during an interview.

Our purpose is to point out some things you can do in advance that will help you and some good rules to follow and pitfalls to avoid while you are being interviewed.

A. *WHAT IS AN INTERVIEW SUPPOSED TO TEST?*

The written examination is designed to test the technical knowledge and competence of the candidate; the oral is designed to evaluate intangible qualities, not readily measured otherwise, and to establish a list showing the relative fitness of each candidate, *as measured against his competitors,* for the position sought. Scoring is not on the basis of "right" or "wrong," but on a sliding scale of values ranging from "not passable" to "outstanding." As a matter of fact, it is possible to achieve a relatively low score without a single "incorrect" answer because of evident weakness in the qualities being measured.

Occasionally, an examination may consist entirely of an oral test -- either an individual or a group oral. In such cases, information is sought concerning the technical knowledges and abilities of the candidate, since there has been no written examination for this purpose. More commonly, however, an oral test is used to supplement a written examination.

B. *WHO CONDUCTS INTERVIEWS?*

The composition of oral boards varies among different jurisdictions. In nearly all, a representative of the personnel department serves as chairman. One of the members of the board may be a representative of the department in which the candidate would work. In some cases, "outside experts" are used, and frequently a business man or some other representative of the general public is asked to serve. Labor and management or other special groups may be represented. The aim is to secure the services of experts in the appropriate field.

However the board is composed, it is a good idea (and not at all improper or unethical) to ascertain in advance of the interview who the members are and what groups they represent. When you are introduced to them, you will have some idea of their backgrounds and interests, and at least you will not stutter and stammer over their names.

C. *WHAT TO DO BEFORE THE INTERVIEW*

While knowledge about the board members is useful and takes some of the surprise element out of the interview, there is other preparation which is more substantive. It *is* possible to prepare for an oral -- in several ways:

1. Keep a Copy of Your Application and Review it Carefully Before the Interview

   This may be the only document before the oral board, and the starting point of the interview. Know what experience and education you have listed there, and the sequence and dates of it. Sometimes the board will ask *you* to review the highlights of your experience for them; you should not have to hem and haw doing it.

2. Study the Class Specification and the Examination Announcement

   Usually, the oral board has one or both of these to guide them. The qualities, characteristics, or knowledges required by the position sought are stated in these documents. They offer valuable clues as to the nature of the oral interview. For example, if the job involves supervisory responsibilities, the announcement will usually indicate that knowledge of modern supervisory methods and the qualifications of the candidate as a supervisor will be tested. If so, you can expect such questions, frequently in the form of a hypothetical situation which you are expected to solve. *Never* go into an oral without knowledge of the duties and responsibilities of the job you seek.

3. Think Through Each Qualification Required

   Try to visualize the kind of questions *you* would ask if you were a board member. How well could you answer them? Try especially to appraise your own knowledge and background in each area, *measured against the job sought,* and identify any areas in which you are weak. Be critical and realistic -- do not flatter yourself.

4. Do Some General Reading in Areas in Which You Feel You May be Weak

   For example, if the job involves supervision and your past experience has *not,* some general reading in supervisory methods and practices, particularly in the field of human relations, might be useful. *Do not* study agency procedures or detailed manuals. The oral board will be testing your understanding and capacity, *not* your memory.

5. Get a Good Night's Sleep and Watch Your General Health and Mental Attitude

   You will want a clear head at the interview. Take care of a cold or other minor ailment, and, of course, *no hangovers.*

D. *WHAT TO DO THE DAY OF THE INTERVIEW*

Now comes the day of the interview itself. Give yourself plenty of time to get there. Plan to arrive somewhat ahead of the scheduled time, particularly if your appointment is in the fore part of the day. If a previous candidate fails to appear, the board might be ready for you a bit early. By early afternoon an oral board is almost invariably behind schedule if there are many candidates, and you may have to wait. Take along a book or magazine to read, or your application to review. But leave any extraneous material in the waiting room when you go in for your interview. In any event, relax and compose yourself.

The matter of dress is important. The board is forming impressions about you -- from your experience, your manners, your attitudes, and from your appearance. Give your personal appearance careful attention. Dress your *best,* but not your flashiest. Choose conservative, appropriate clothing, and be sure it and you are immaculate. This is a business interview, and your appearance should indicate that you regard it as such. Besides, being well-groomed and properly dressed will help boost your confidence.

Sooner or later, someone will call your name and escort you into the interview room. *This is it.* From here on you are on your own. It is too late for any more preparation. But, remember, you asked for this opportunity to prove your fitness, and you are here because your request was granted.

E. *WHAT HAPPENS WHEN YOU GO IN?*

The usual sequence of events will be as follows: The clerk (who is often the board stenographer) will introduce you to the chairman of the oral board, who will introduce you to each other member of the board. Acknowledge the introductions before you sit down. Do not be surprised if you find a microphone facing you or a stenotypist sitting by. Oral interviews are usually recorded, in the event of an appeal or other review.

Usually the chairman of the board will open the interview by reviewing the highlights of your education and work experience from your application -- primarily for the benefit of the other members of the board, as well as to get the material into the record. Do not interrupt or comment unless there is an error or significant misinterpretation; if so, do not hesitate. But do not quibble about insignificant matters. Usually, also, he will ask you some question about your education, your experience, or your present job -- partly to get you started talking, to establish the interviewing "rapport." He may start the actual questioning, or turn it over to one of the other members. Frequently each member undertakes the questioning on a particular area, one in which he is perhaps most competent. So you can expect each member to participate in the examination. And because the time is limited, you may expect some rather abrupt switches in the direction the questioning takes. Do not be upset by it. Normally, a board member will not pursue a single line of questioning unless he discovers a particular strength or weakness.

After each member has participated, the chairman will usually ask whether any member has any further questions, then will ask you if you have anything you wish to add. Unless you are expecting this question, it may floor you. Or worse, it may start you off on an extended, extemporaneous speech. The board is not usually seeking more information. The question is principally to offer you a last opportunity to present further qualifications or to indicate that you have nothing to add. So, if you feel that a significant qualification or characteristic has been overlooked, it is proper to point it out in a sentence or so. Do not compliment the board on the thoroughness of their examination -- they have been sketchy, and you know it. If you wish, merely say, "No thank you, I have nothing further to add." This is a point where you can "talk yourself out" of a good impression or fail to present an important bit of information. *Remember, you close the interview yourself.*

The chairman will then say,"That is all,Mr.Smith,thank you." Do not be startled; the interview is over, and quicker than you think. Say,"Thank you and good morning," gather up your belongings and take your leave. Save your sigh of relief for the other side of the door.

F. HOW TO PUT YOUR BEST FOOT FORWARD

Throughout all this process, you may feel that the board individually and collectively is trying to pierce your defenses, to seek out your hidden weaknesses, and to embarrass and confuse you. Actually, this is not true. They are obliged to make an appraisal of your qualifications for the job you are seeking, and they *want to see you in your best light*. Remember, they must interview all candidates and a noncooperative candidate may become a failure in spite of their best efforts to bring out his qualifications. Here are fifteen(15) suggestions that will help you:

1. Be Natural. Keep Your Attitude Confident,But Not Cocky

If *you* are not confident that you can do the job, do not expect the *board* to be. Do not apologize for your weaknesses, try to bring out your strong points. The board is interested in a positive, not a negative presentation. Cockiness will antagonize any board member, and make him wonder if you are covering up a weakness by a false show of strength.

2. Get Comfortable, But Don't Lounge or Sprawl

Sit erectly but not stiffly. A careless posture may lead the board to conclude you are careless in other things, or at least that you are not impressed by the importance of the occasion to you.Either conclusion is natural, even if incorrect. Do not fuss with your clothing, or with a pencil or an ashtray. Your hands may occasionally be useful to emphasize a point; do not let them become a point of distraction.

3. Do Not Wisecrack or Make Small Talk

This is a serious situation, and your attitude should show that you consider it as such. Further, the time of the board is limited; they do not want to waste it, and neither should you.

4. Do Not Exaggerate Your Experience or Abilities

In the first place, from information in the application,from other interviews and other sources, the board may know more about you than you think; in the second place, you probably will not get away with it in the first place. An experienced board is rather adept at spotting such a situation. Do not take the chance.

5. If You Know a Member of the Board, Do Not Make a Point of It, Yet Do Not Hide It.

Certainly you are not fooling him, and probably not the other members of the board. Do not try to take advantage of your acquaintanceship -- it will probably do you little good.

6. Do Not Dominate the Interview

Let the board do that. They will give you the clues -- do not assume that you have to do all the talking. Realize that the board has a number of questions to ask you, and do not try to take up all the interview time by showing off your extensive knowledge of the answer to the first one.

15

7. Be Attentive

You only have twenty minutes or so, and you should keep your attention at its sharpest throughout. When a member is addressing a problem or a question to you, give him your undivided attention. Address your reply principally to him, but do not exclude the other members of the board.

8. Do Not Interrupt

A board member may be stating a problem for you to analyze. He will ask you a question when the time comes. Let him state the problem, and wait for the question.

9. Make Sure You Understand the Question

Do not try to answer until you are sure what the question is. If it is not clear, restate it in your own words or ask the board member to clarify it for you. But do not haggle about minor elements.

10. Reply Promptly But Not Hastily

A common entry on oral board rating sheets is "candidate responded readily," or "candidate hesitated in replies." Respond as promptly and quickly as you can, but do not jump to a hasty, ill-considered answer.

11. Do Not Be Peremptory in Your Answers

A brief answer is proper -- but do not fire your answer back. That is a losing game from your point of view. The board member can probably ask questions much faster than you can answer them.

12. Do Not Try To Create the Answer You Think the Board Member Wants

He is interested in what kind of mind you have and how it works -- not in playing games. Furthermore, he can usually spot this practice and will usually grade you down on it.

13. Do Not Switch Sides in Your Reply Merely to Agree With a Board Member

Frequently, a member will take a contrary position merely to draw you out and to see if you are willing and able to defend your point of view. Do not start a debate, yet do not surrender a good position. If a position is worth taking, it is worth defending.

14. Do Not Be Afraid to Admit an Error in Judgment if You Are Shown to Be Wrong

The board knows that you are forced to reply without any opportunity for careful consideration. Your answer may be demonstrably wrong. If so, admit it and get on with the interview.

15. Do Not Dwell at Length on Your Present Job

The opening question may relate to your present assignment. Answer the question but do not go into an extended discussion. You are being examined for a *new* job, not your present one. As a matter of fact, try to phrase *all* your answers in terms of the job for which you are being examined.

G. BASIS OF RATING

Probably you will forget most of these "do's" and "don'ts" when you walk into the oral interview room. Even remembering them all will not insure you a passing grade. Perhaps you did not have the qualifications in the first place. But remembering them *will* help you to put your best foot forward, without treading on the toes of the board members.

Rumor and popular opinion to the contrary notwithstanding, an oral board wants you to make the best appearance possible. They know you are under pressure -- but they also want to see how you respond to it as a guide to what your reaction would be under the pressures of the job you seek. They will be influenced by the degree of poise you display, the personal traits you show, and the manner in which you respond.

EXAMINATION SECTION

EXAMINATION SECTION
TEST 1

DIRECTIONS: Each question or incomplete statement is followed by several suggested answers or completions. Select the one that BEST answers the question or completes the statement. *PRINT THE LETTER OF THE CORRECT ANSWER IN THE SPACE AT THE RIGHT.*

Questions 1-3.

DIRECTIONS: Questions 1 through 3 are to be answered SOLELY on the basis of the following paragraph.

Helping to prevent accidents is the job of every worker. Tell your foreman about unsafe equipment right away. Wear safe clothing. Bend your knees when lifting and get somebody to help you with very heavy objects.

1. The above passage says that helping to prevent accidents   1.___
   is the job of
     A. the foreman   B. the safety division
     C. management   D. every worker

2. Equipment that is not safe should be   2.___
     A. used with special care
     B. reported to your foreman right away
     C. marked with a red tag
     D. parked at the side of the road

3. When lifting very heavy objects, you should   3.___
     A. ask your foreman to see what you are doing
     B. keep your legs straight
     C. always wear protective gloves
     D. get somebody to help you

4. Sanitation men are expected to do the work they are   4.___
   assigned to do. In addition, however, they are expected
   to have good relations with the public in order to
   reduce the likelihood of complaints.
   According to the above statement, good relations with the
   public is DESIRABLE because
     A. it may reduce the number of complaints
     B. sanitation men are highly qualified
     C. a worker's personality is important on the job
     D. public relations is the most important part of the
        job of a sanitation man

5. People who do not work with their hands do not know how   5.___
   hard it is to do manual work.
   According to the above statement, manual work is work
   which is
     A. not hard to do   B. done by many people
     C. done with the hands   D. understood by few people

Questions 6-8.

DIRECTIONS: Questions 6 through 8 are to be answered SOLELY on the
               basis of the following paragraph.

A heavy snowfall may cause delays in the movement of trains and
buses. People are often late for work when it snows. Both pedestrians and cars have accidents because of snow and ice. Pedestrians
slip and fall. Cars skid and collide.

6.   The above passage indicates that heavy snow   6.___
      A. is a beautiful thing to see
      B. may make the trains run late
      C. gives temporary work to the unemployed
      D. should be cleared from sidewalks within four hours

7.   According to the above passage, snow and ice may cause   7.___
      cars to
      A. slow down B. freeze   C. stall   D. skid

8.   The above passage says that when it snows,   8.___
      A. children love to have snowball fights
      B. people are often late for work
      C. garbage collection is halted
      D. snow plows must be attached to garbage trucks

Questions 9-10.

DIRECTIONS: Questions 9 and 10 are to be answered SOLELY on the
               basis of the following paragraph.

It would be unusual for a snowstorm to develop without warning.
When a warning is received, sanitation men load the salt spreaders
and attach plows to the trucks.

9.   According to the above paragraph, a snowstorm seldom   9.___
      develops
      A. without advance notice   B. in the spring
      C. in the city   D. without rain coming first

10.   Once a snow warning is received, sanitation men prepare   10.___
      for the storm by
      A. removing plows from the trucks
      B. greasing and oiling the salt spreaders
      C. emptying the salt spreaders
      D. putting plows on the trucks

11.   Because trucks are heavier than cars, they are more   11.___
      difficult to slow down and stop.
      According to this statement, the reason trucks are MORE
      difficult to stop than cars is that
      A. cars are slower than trucks
      B. cars usually have automatic shift

C. trucks are more likely to stall
D. trucks weigh more than cars

Questions 12-21.

DIRECTIONS: Questions 12 through 21 test your understanding of the words italicized in each question.

12. The large *vehicle* was being repaired.   12.___
    Which of the following is a *vehicle*?
        A. Truck   B. Building   C. Boiler   D. Table

13. The *fence* needs to be painted.   13.___
    The one of the following which is MOST like a *fence* is a
        A. door   B. crane   C. wall   D. building

14. *Furniture* is not taken with the regular collection.   14.___
    Which of the following is *furniture*?
        A. Sofas and chairs   B. Cars and trucks
        C. Brooms and mops   D. Bags and boxes

15. The *group* was assigned to do special work.   15.___
    Which of the following is a *group*?
        A. Truck   B. Boat   C. Team   D. Foreman

16. Sanitation men often use *tools* in their work.   16.___
    The one of the following which is MOST often considered
    a *tool* is a
        A. tire   B. shovel   C. glove   D. basket

17. The man claimed that he could not *lift* the can.   17.___
    The word *lift* means MOST NEARLY
        A. bury   B. pick up   C. refill   D. clean

18. Place all the boxes *below* the second shelf.   18.___
    The word *below* means
        A. under   B. into   C. beside   D. over

19. The truck could not go under the bridge because the   19.___
    bridge was too *low*.
    The reason the truck could not go under the bridge was
    that the bridge was not _____ enough.
        A. high   B. long   C. strong   D. wide

20. He could not get his truck on the *highway*.   20.___
    A *highway* is a type of
        A. lot   B. road   C. scale   D. sidewalk

21. This street should be *clean* when the sanitation men   21.___
    finish.
    The word *clean* means free of
        A. obstacles   B. pedestrians
        C. traffic   D. dirt

22. Even minor injuries on the job should be reported to one's   22.____
    supervisor and should be treated by a doctor if necessary.
    According to this statement, all injuries on the job
        A. are usually minor
        B. should be reported to one's supervisor
        C. should be treated by a doctor
        D. can be avoided

23. Up to the age of forty, people in good health should have   23.____
    a medical check-up once a year. People over 40 should
    have a check-up twice a year. People in poor health
    should have a check-up even more frequently.
    According to this statement, people under 40 who are in
    good health should have a medical check-up _____ year.
        A. once a
        B. twice a
        C. more frequently than twice a
        D. once every other

24. After stopping a sanitation truck, it is very important   24.____
    that you look out for children just before stepping on
    the gas pedal again.
    According to this statement, it is necessary to look out
    for children
        A. after putting a sanitation truck in motion
        B. immediately after stopping a sanitation truck
        C. immediately before stepping on the gas pedal
        D. before stopping a sanitation truck

Questions 25-30.

DIRECTIONS: In each of Questions 25 through 30, there is a sign
             with four choices at the right. Look at the sign
             and then print the letter that BEST describes the
             meaning of the sign in the space at the right.

25. <u>YIELD AHEAD</u>   This sign tells you to   25.____
                                  A. give up the right-of-way ahead
                                  B. turn right ahead
                                  C. increase your speed ahead
                                  D. park your vehicle ahead

26. <u>SLIPPERY</u>   This sign tells you that when the   26.____
       <u>WHEN</u>   road is wet
       <u>WET</u>   A. your vehicle may stall
                                  B. your vehicle may slide
                                  C. the pavement may crack
                                  D. you may not use this road

27. STREET
    CLOSED
    1000 FT.

    This sign tells you that, about 1,000 feet ahead, the street
       A. is dangerous
       B. curves to the right
       C. is not open
       D. becomes a highway

    27.____

28. REDUCED
    SPEED
    AHEAD

    This sign tells you that further ahead you must
       A. go slower
       B. go faster
       C. continue at the same speed
       D. make a left turn

    28.____

29. NO
    TURNS

    This sign tells you that you must
       A. go straight ahead
       B. stay in your lane
       C. not pass another car
       D. not slow down

    29.____

30. DO NOT
    ENTER

    This sign tells you that you must NOT
       A. go in
       B. speed up
       C. slow down
       D. stop

    30.____

KEY (CORRECT ANSWERS)

1.	D	11.	D	21.	D
2.	B	12.	A	22.	B
3.	D	13.	C	23.	A
4.	A	14.	A	24.	C
5.	C	15.	C	25.	A
6.	B	16.	B	26.	B
7.	D	17.	B	27.	C
8.	B	18.	A	28.	A
9.	A	19.	A	29.	A
10.	D	20.	B	30.	A

TEST 2

DIRECTIONS: Each question or incomplete statement is followed by several suggested answers or completions. Select the one that BEST answers the question or completes the statement. *PRINT THE LETTER OF THE CORRECT ANSWER IN THE SPACE AT THE RIGHT.*

Questions 1-2.

DIRECTIONS: Questions 1 and 2 are to be answered SOLELY on the basis of the following passage.

The Department of Sanitation starts early in the month of May to prepare for snow expected during the following winter. It begins by fixing the snow removal equipment which was used during the winter. It is then usually kept busy with either snow removal or preparation for snow removal every month through the end of March.

1. According to the above passage, for how many months during the year is the Department of Sanitation busy with either snow removal or preparation for snow removal?
   A. 9　　　　　B. 10　　　　　C. 11　　　　　D. 12　　　　　1.___

2. According to the above passage, in the month of May the Department of Sanitation　　　　　2.___
   A. stores the snow removal equipment
   B. fixes the snow removal equipment
   C. equips the sanitation men
   D. collects the garbage piled up because of snow

Questions 3-12.

DIRECTIONS: In Questions 3 through 12, pick the lettered answer which means MOST NEARLY the same as the italicized word in the sentence.

3. The sanitation men *combined* the contents of the two boxes. The word *combined* means　　　　　3.___
   A. sifted through　　　　B. put together
   C. tore apart　　　　　　D. forgot about

4. Don't touch the *lever* on the left side. The word *lever* means　　　　　4.___
   A. button　　　B. rope　　　C. handle　　　D. gun

5. All *litter* should be taken away. The word *litter* means　　　　　5.___
   A. paint　　　B. bowls　　　C. rubbish　　　D. evidence

6. The *inspection* of the street was complete.   6.___
   The word *inspection* means
      A. cleaning   B. examination
      C. repair   D. painting

7. The *route* must be followed exactly.   7.___
   The word *route* means
      A. foreman   B. truck   C. way   D. recipe

8. Don't *injure* your back.   8.___
   The word *injure* means
      A. bend   B. use   C. hurt   D. exercise

9. John *repaired* the machine.   9.___
   The word *repaired* means
      A. fixed   B. broke   C. ran   D. oiled

10. Put the *lid* on the box.   10.___
    The word *lid* means
       A. cover   B. ribbon   C. rope   D. wrapping

11. The *rear* of the truck should be washed.   11.___
    The word *rear* means
       A. hood   B. front   C. back   D. roof

12. Sanitation men must *assist* each other while at work.   12.___
    The word *assist* means
       A. help   B. outdo   C. like   D. hurt

Questions 13-18.

DIRECTIONS: Questions 13 through 18 are to be answered by performing the operation required (addition or subtraction).

13. Add: 10,487   13.___
          + 145

       A. 10,342   B. 10,622   C. 10,632   D. 10,652

14. Add: 26,836   14.___
          +   87

       A. 26,749   B. 26,923   C. 26,943   D. 26,973

15. Subtract: 83,204   15.___
              -83,075

       A. 109   B. 129   C. 139   D. 144

16. Subtract: 19,095   16.___
              -19,029

       A. 66   B. 74   C. 79   D. 86

17. If the mileage indicator on your truck reads 14,382 at
    the beginning of the day and it reads 14,431 at the end
    of the day, the number of miles that the truck has been
    driven that day is
      A. 29   B. 34   C. 39   D. 49

17. ___

18. On a certain day, your truck makes three trips to the
    dumping area and dumps 5.5 tons, 6.3 tons, and 4.8 tons
    of trash.
    The TOTAL number of tons of trash that the truck has
    dumped that day is
      A. 15.0   B. 15.6   C. 16.0   D. 16.6

18. ___

Questions 19-23.

DIRECTIONS: Assume that, while driving a Department of Sanitation
            vehicle, you have been involved in an accident and
            that you are required to fill out an Accident Report
            form. Questions 19 through 23 are to be answered on
            the basis of the following Accident Report form.

ACCIDENT REPORT	
Block #1 DATE AND TIME Date of Accident _____ Time of Accident _____	Block #2 LOCATION OF ACCIDENT
Block #3 DEPARTMENT OF SANITATION VEHICLE Operator's Name _____ Operator's License No. _____ Vehicle License No. _____	Block #4 OTHER VEHICLE Vehicle License # _____ Owner's Name _____ Operator's Name _____ Operator's License No. _____
Block #5 TYPE OF ACCIDENT Head On ___ Front End ___ Side Swipe ___ Non-Collision ___ Right Angle ___	Block #6 LIGHT CONDITION Daylight ___ Dusk ___ Dark ___ Dawn ___

Block #7 TYPE OF TRAFFIC CONTROL
         NEAREST TO LOCATION OF
              ACCIDENT
Police Officer ___ Stop Sign ___
Crossing Guard ___ Yield Sign ___
Traffic Light ___
	Block #8 ROAD TYPE
	One-Way ___ Separated ___
	Two-Way ___ Not Separated ___

Block #9 WEATHER CONDITIONS Clear ___ Fog ___ Raining ___ Snowing ___ Sleeting ___	Block #10 ROAD SURFACE AND CONDITION Black-Top ___ Wet ___ Concrete ___ Dry ___
Block #11 JOB BEING PERFORMED AT TIME OF ACCIDENT Driving Along Collection Route ___ Stopped, Loading Along Route ___ Driving to Dumping Area ___ Other ___	

19. The accident took place at the corner of Jerome Avenue   19.___
    and 170th Street.
    On the form, you should write *the corner of Jerome Avenue*
    and 170th Street in the block entitled
       A. LOCATION OF ACCIDENT   B. TYPE OF ACCIDENT
       C. WEATHER CONDITIONS   D. LIGHT CONDITIONS

20. The accident happened when the sides of both vehicles   20.___
    came into contact as the other driver was trying to
    pass you.
    On the form, in the block entitled TYPE OF ACCIDENT, you
    should check the box marked
       A. Head On   B. Side Swipe
       C. Right Angle   D. Front End

21. At the location of the accident, a police officer was   21.___
    directing traffic.
    The proper place on the form for this information is the
    block entitled
       A. TYPE OF TRAFFIC CONTROL NEAREST TO LOCATION OF
          ACCIDENT
       B. TYPE OF ACCIDENT
       C. JOB BEING PERFORMED AT TIME OF ACCIDENT
       D. ROAD SURFACE AND CONDITION

22. Since the accident happened at 11:00 P.M., you should   22.___
    write *11:00 P.M.* in Block #
       A. 1   B. 3   C. 5   D. 7

23. On the street where the accident happened, all traffic   23.___
    had to go in the same direction.
    On the form, in the block entitled ROAD TYPE, you should
    check the box next to
       A. Not Separated   B. Two-Way
       C. Separated   D. One-Way

Questions 24-27.

DIRECTIONS: Questions 24 through 27 are to be answered based on the
              Accident Report form shown for Questions 19 through 23.

24. When the accident happened, it was raining, and you were   24.___
    on a blacktop street.
    On the form, in the block entitled ROAD SURFACE AND CON-
    DITION, you should check the two boxes next to
       A. Wet and Concrete   B. Dry and Concrete
       C. Wet and Blacktop   D. Dry and Blacktop

25. When the accident happened, you were driving along your   25.___
    collection route.
    You should put this information in the block entitled
       A. ROAD SURFACE AND CONDITION
       B. LOCATION OF ACCIDENT
       C. TYPE OF TRAFFIC CONTROL NEAREST TO THE LOCATION
       D. JOB BEING PERFORMED AT TIME OF ACCIDENT

26. The accident happened on March 2, 1990.   26.____
    On the form, you should write *March 2, 1990* in Block #
    A. 1   B. 4   C. 7   D. 10

27. The name of the other person involved in the accident   27.____
    is Frank Smith.
    On the form, you should put this information in the
    block entitled
    A. JOB BEING PERFORMED AT TIME OF ACCIDENT
    B. LOCATION OF ACCIDENT
    C. TYPE OF TRAFFIC CONTROL NEAREST TO LOCATION
    D. OTHER VEHICLE

Questions 28-30.

DIRECTIONS: Questions 28 through 30 are to be answered SOLELY on
               the basis of the information in the following passage.

    Sanitation men sometimes have to listen to complaints from the
public. When an angry citizen complains to you, you should remember
to stay calm. If you can answer the complaint, you should do so.
If you cannot answer the complaint, you should refer the citizen to
someone who can answer it.

28. Sanitation men who come into contact with the public   28.____
    sometimes have to
    A. sweep up trash   B. shout at citizens
    C. listen to complaints   D. help put out fires

29. If a citizen who is complaining to you is very angry, you   29.____
    should
    A. get angry
    B. stay calm
    C. ignore him
    D. tell him to leave you alone

30. If you cannot answer the complaint, you should   30.____
    A. make up something that sounds logical
    B. ask a passerby for the information
    C. tell him who can give him the answer
    D. tell him you do not know and walk away

KEY (CORRECT ANSWERS)

1. C	11. C	21. A
2. B	12. A	22. A
3. B	13. C	23. D
4. C	14. B	24. C
5. C	15. B	25. D
6. B	16. A	26. A
7. C	17. D	27. D
8. C	18. D	28. C
9. A	19. A	29. B
10. A	20. B	30. C

EXAMINATION SECTION

TEST 1

DIRECTIONS: Each question or incomplete statement is followed by several suggested answers or completions. Select the one that BEST answers the question or completes the statement. *PRINT THE LETTER OF THE CORRECT ANSWER IN THE SPACE AT THE RIGHT.*

1. Before the average snow plow can be brought to a complete stop from a speed of 20 miles per hour, it will travel approximately 40 feet.
Based on this statement, it would PROBABLY be unsafe to drive a snow plow at
    A. more than 20 miles per hour at any time
    B. 20 miles per hour if the plow stops in less than average distance
    C. more than 20 miles per hour unless the driver can stop the plow within approximately 40 feet
    D. 20 miles per hour if the driver cannot see the road 40 feet ahead of him

              1.____

2. Of the following, which is the MOST likely reason why so many traffic accidents occur between the hours of 5 P.M. and 9 P.M.?
    A. Visibility is generally poorer during these hours.
    B. Those who drive at these hours are generally not as experienced as those who drive during the day.
    C. Those who drive at these hours are generally not as experienced as those who drive at night.
    D. People are more anxious to get home than to get to work.

              2.____

3. Suppose you are assigned to drive a sanitation truck and given the key to the vehicle by your foreman. When you get into the vehicle, you make several attempts to insert the key into the ignition but are unable to do so.
It would be BEST for you to FIRST
    A. check with your foreman that he gave you the correct key
    B. rub some powdered graphite on the key
    C. squeeze some powdered graphite into the ignition lock
    D. use a little more pressure and *jiggle* the key around a bit

              3.____

4. Accidents can be caused by either an unsafe act or an unsafe condition.
The one of the following which is an example of an unsafe condition, rather than of an unsafe act, is
    A. use of defective tools
    B. refusal to wear required protective clothing
    C. poor steering mechanism in a vehicle
    D. careless lifting of heavy objects

              4.____

5. For a sanitation man to consciously obey routine safety   5.___
   rules of the Department so that they become definite
   habits is
   A. *bad* because conscious habits are ineffective
   B. *good* because habits are not often forgotten
   C. *bad* because habits are rarely formed consciously
   D. *good* because routine rules are usually unimportant

6. Accidents often happen because a person lets his mind   6.___
   wander while working.
   From this, if it is true, it MUST follow that
   A. it pays for a person to keep his mind on his work
   B. carelessness usually leads to an accident
   C. anything worth doing at all is worth doing well
   D. accidents are a chief cause of poor work

7. The Health Code provides that all *receptacles for removal*   7.___
   of waste material...shall be provided with tight-fitting
   metal covers.
   The MOST probable reason for this is to prevent
   A. accumulation of rainwater or snow
   B. escape of foul odors
   C. overloading of cans
   D. spillage of material

8. Suppose that while you are working as a sanitation man on   8.___
   your route, a very excited building superintendent asks you
   where he can see your foreman. He refuses to tell you why
   he wants to see him.
   You should tell him
   A. you will not give him any information until he tells
      you why he wants to see your foreman
   B. why your foreman does not have the time for personal
      interviews with everyone
   C. where he can see your foreman and at what hours
   D. he'll have to calm down before you will talk to him
      further

9. Of the following, the MAIN reason for having an official   9.___
   bulletin board at a job location is to
   A. train the employees in the important parts of their
      jobs
   B. make it easier for union organizations to contact
      their members
   C. list the names of new personnel and those recently
      retired
   D. inform employees of new orders and procedures

10. A MAJOR reason why written orders are sometimes given to   10.___
    employees instead of oral orders is that
    A. written orders should be carried out ahead of oral
       orders
    B. unnecessary orders will not be given if they must
       be issued in writing

C. details of orders are less likely to be forgotten if written out
D. a superior's written orders are more easily understood by the average employee

11. If a homeowner asks you why his garbage is not picked up on time, you should tell him 11.___
   A. the reason if you know it
   B. he gets the same service as everybody else
   C. to write a letter to your Department
   D. you do not know in order to avoid an argument

12. Which one of the following is a POOR reason for not allowing sanitation men to accept Christmas presents or other tips from the public? 12.___
   A. Taking tips may influence the sanitation man to give poorer service to those who don't tip.
   B. The public will think they must give tips to get good service.
   C. The public is entitled to service without giving tips.
   D. It is an old American custom to give Christmas presents or tips to those who serve you.

13. In judging the work of a sanitation man assigned manual sweeping of streets, the number of streets swept is an important factor. 13.___
   Of the following factors, the NEXT in importance would be the
   A. character of the residents
   B. condition of the streets after sweeping is completed
   C. number of complaints received from the public
   D. time of year at which the sweeping is done

14. Suppose that you were appointed a sanitation man before A, and A was appointed after B. 14.___
   Then, the MOST correct statement about the order of the three appointments, based ONLY on the above information, is that
   A. B may have been appointed before you or after you
   B. B was appointed after you
   C. you were appointed first, B was appointed next
   D. you were the first to be appointed

15. To be appointed a sanitation man, a person must be in good physical condition. 15.___
   Of the following, the LEAST important reason for this requirement is that sanitation men
   A. are seen by the general public
   B. do heavy lifting
   C. often do considerable walking on their jobs
   D. work outdoors in all kinds of weather

16. While you are working as part of a collection truck crew,   16.___
    a building owner complains to you that one of his cans
    has been dented by a sanitation man in another collection
    crew.
    From the point of view of good public relations, it would
    be BEST if you
    A. inquired how long he had the can and if it wasn't
       just normal wear and tear
    B. expressed the regrets of the Department and asked
       whether perhaps the can was packed too tightly with
       material
    C. explained why a certain amount of damage is unavoid-
       able
    D. explained that the damage might have been done by
       some youngsters as a prank

17. A sanitation man will MOST likely create the best *image* of   17.___
    the Department of Sanitation in the mind of the public if
    he
    A. answers all questions asked of him
    B. avoids arguments
    C. does his job well
    D. *minds his own business*

Questions 18-34.

DIRECTIONS: Questions 18 through 34, inclusive, consist of a word
               in capital letters followed by four suggested meanings
               of the word. Indicate the word or phrase which means
               MOST NEARLY the same as the word in capitals.

18. VARIOUS   18.___
    A. dangerous B. noisy   C. outdoor   D. several

19. AMBIGUOUS   19.___
    A. alike   B. not clear C. short   D. very eager

20. PRECISELY   20.___
    A. costly   B. poorly   C. in advance D. exactly

21. STURDY   21.___
    A. dark   B. learn   C. read   D. strong

22. RESPONSE   22.___
    A. rest   B. suit   C. answer   D. breathe

23. RESCIND   23.___
    A. burn up   B. cancel   C. do again   D. grow

24. ASSISTANCE   24.___
    A. case   B. gift   C. help   D. move

25. CONSUME   25.___
     A. want   B. use up
     C. sell   D. add together

26. HAZARDOUS   26.___
     A. annoying   B. causing   C. foggy   D. risky

27. DECELERATE   27.___
     A. slow down   B. speed up
     C. walk down   D. walk up

28. SUBSEQUENTLY   28.___
     A. wisely   B. stupidly   C. before   D. afterward

29. DECOMPOSE   29.___
     A. choose   B. get control
     C. pick up   D. rot

30. RESTRICT   30.___
     A. hit again   B. limit   C. sit down   D. soften

31. AUGMENT   31.___
     A. stop   B. start   C. increase   D. disagree

32. UTILIZE   32.___
     A. find fault with   B. give praise to
     C. put to use   D. try to improve

33. TOXIC   33.___
     A. usual   B. poisonous
     C. improved   D. abnormal

34. SUFFICIENT   34.___
     A. hurt   B. enough   C. choke   D. better

35. A driver who extends his hand and arm out the window in a   35.___
horizontal position is giving the legal hand signal for
     A. a left turn   B. a right turn
     C. slowing down   D. stopping

36. For a driver to keep the clutch engaged when he is in a   36.___
skid is a _____ practice because _____.
     A. *poor*; it lessens the driver's control
     B. *good*; it helps reduce the speed
     C. *poor*; it makes the skid worse
     D. *good*; it prevents stripping the gears

37. To make a left turn from a two-lane one-way road into   37.___
another two-lane one-way road, a driver should, if
possible, approach the turn in the _____-hand lane and
turn into the _____-hand lane of the road he is entering.
     A. right; left   B. left; left
     C. right; right   D. left; right

38. When approaching a curve in the road while driving, you   38.___
    should ____ before entering the curve and ____ while
    in the curve.
        A. increase your speed slightly; slow down
        B. maintain the same speed; increase your speed slightly
        C. slow down; continue decreasing your speed
        D. slow down; increase your speed slightly

39. When passing a vehicle coming from the opposite direction   39.___
    at night, a driver should fix his eyes
        A. straight ahead
        B. on the center line of the road
        C. on the right-hand side of the road
        D. on the left-hand side of the road

40. When driving in dense fog, it is BEST to use the ____   40.___
    beam of the headlights and keep as ____ .
        A. low; close as possible to the center line
        B. high; close as possible to the center line
        C. low; far to the right of the center line as possible
        D. high; far to the right of the center line as possible

41. The PROPER immediate first aid care for a frostbitten hand   41.___
    is to
        A. rub the hand with snow
        B. place the part in warm water
        C. cover the hand with a woolen cloth
        D. vigorously rub the hands together

42. The symptoms of heat exhaustion are -   42.___
        A. pale, clammy skin, low temperature, weak pulse
        B. rapid and strong pulse, dry skin, high temperature
        C. headache, red face, unconsciousness
        D. abdominal cramps, red skin, profuse sweating

43. Arterial pressure points   43.___
        A. are best located by taking the pulse
        B. lie close to bones near the surface of the body
        C. are used to cut off all blood circulation
        D. are deep-seated and require great pressure

44. Of the following, the one NOT recommended for the first   44.___
    aid care of burns is
        A. boric acid   B. baking soda
        C. petrolatum ointment   D. Epsom salts

45. A person who has fainted should be   45.___
        A. propped up on a pillow or head rest
        B. given a warm drink
        C. aroused as soon as possible
        D. laid flat and kept quiet

46. Of the following associations of symptom(s) and sudden
    illness or accident, the INCORRECT one is
    A. blood spurting from the wrist - cut artery
    B. stoppage of breathing - suffocation
    C. pale, cold, moist skin - shock
    D. partial tearing of ligaments of a joint - strain

46.___

47. In the care of a sprained ankle, an INCORRECT procedure
    in first aid would be to
    A. elevate the sprained part
    B. apply cold applications
    C. massage the part to restore circulation
    D. apply a temporary support

47.___

48. In administering first aid, one should encourage bleeding
    by mild pressure, being careful not to bruise the tissue,
    in wounds classified as
    A. punctures   B. incisions
    C. lacerations   D. abrasions

48.___

49. All of the following first aid rules for simple nosebleed
    may be safely followed EXCEPT
    A. gently pinching the nostrils together
    B. applying cold compresses to the nose
    C. blowing the nose gently after bleeding stops to remove
       blood clots
    D. inserting a plug of absorbent cotton in each of the
       nostrils

49.___

50. Of the following associations of symptom and illness, the
    one which is NOT correct is
    A. cough - onset of measles
    B. pallor - anemia
    C. sore throat - impetigo
    D. red eyes, accompanied by a discharge - conjunctivitis

50.___

KEY (CORRECT ANSWERS)

1. D	11. A	21. D	31. C	41. C
2. A	12. D	22. C	32. C	42. A
3. A	13. B	23. B	33. B	43. B
4. C	14. A	24. C	34. B	44. A
5. B	15. A	25. B	35. A	45. D
6. A	16. B	26. D	36. B	46. D
7. D	17. C	27. A	37. B	47. C
8. C	18. D	28. D	38. D	48. A
9. D	19. B	29. D	39. C	49. C
10. C	20. D	30. B	40. C	50. C

TEST 2

DIRECTIONS: Each question or incomplete statement is followed by several suggested answers or completions. Select the one that BEST answers the question or completes the statement. *PRINT THE LETTER OF THE CORRECT ANSWER IN THE SPACE AT THE RIGHT.*

1. The ammeter on the instrument panel of a motor vehicle normally should show DISCHARGE when
    A. the motor is being started
    B. the engine is running rapidly
    C. the water level in the battery is above the battery plates
    D. all electrical switches are off

    1.___

2. As the pistons move downward in a gasoline engine, they cause a rotating movement of the
    A. spark plugs   B. crankshaft
    C. carburetor   D. air cleaner

    2.___

3. When may a driver stop his car temporarily in front of a *No Standing* traffic sign?
    A. Only if the car is disabled
    B. Only to let fire apparatus pass
    C. To load or unload merchandise
    D. To receive or discharge passengers

    3.___

4. When the yellow light goes on in a three-colored traffic light at an intersection, it means that a driver approaching the intersection
    A. should realize that the red light will come in seconds
    B. must be cautious going through the intersection
    C. may enter the intersection only if making a right-hand turn
    D. is not allowed to enter the intersection

    4.___

5. A diamond-shaped highway sign which shows an arrow curving sharply to the right is warning that
    A. there is a sharp turn ahead in the road
    B. there is a sharp narrowing of the road ahead
    C. there may be traffic ahead entering on the right
    D. a steep hill is ahead

    5.___

6. When giving first aid to a seriously injured accident victim, treatment for shock should be included MAINLY because
    A. there are no easily recognizable symptoms of shock
    B. symptoms of shock only appear hours after the accident
    C. shock occurs to some degree after every serious injury
    D. a victim of shock will die if not treated immediately

    6.___

7. If a Department of Sanitation truck is involved in a   7.___
serious traffic accident, which one of the following items
is it LEAST important to include in the report of the
accident?
   A. The name of the other party's lawyer
   B. The names of all witnesses
   C. The probable cause of the accident
   D. The time of the accident

8. An injured person should be kept lying down. If he begins   8.___
to vomit, his head should be turned to one side.
The MAIN reason for turning the head to one side is to
   A. control the spread of germs
   B. stop the nausea
   C. reduce the area of soiled clothing
   D. help prevent choking

9. A person who is confident he can complete a task is said   9.___
to be
   A. courageous   B. sure
   C. bright   D. successful

10. If a child sleeping peacefully is awakened by a sudden   10.___
cry, he is likely to be
   A. ill   B. uncomfortable
   C. startled   D. hungry

11. A bank is to money as a _____ is to books.   11.___
   A. authors   B. building
   C. library   D. librarian

12. The shortest distance between two points is a(n)   12.___
   A. cross-section   B. straight line
   C. angle   D. drawing

13. No time was set for the conference.   13.___
The word below that BEST describes this fact is
   A. indefinite   B. decisive
   C. ignored   D. powerful

14. A person who is influenced in making a decision by pre-   14.___
conceived opinions is said to be
   A. subjective   B. obstinate
   C. hateful   D. ignorant

15. The opposite of extravagant is   15.___
   A. affluent B. costly   C. frugal   D. cheap

16. A dinner always involves   16.___
   A. service B. waitress C. cloth   D. food

Questions 17-24.

DIRECTIONS: Questions 17 through 24 are to be answered SOLELY on
               the basis of the information given in the following
               passage.

Machine flushing is the process of washing the street and forcibly
pushing the street dirt toward the curbs by directing streams of water
under pressure onto the surface of the street from a moving vehicle.
Flushers have been known to clean as little as 1½ miles and as much
as 41 miles of street during a single eight-hour shift. The average
for an eight-hour shift, as shown in a survey made of 36 cities, is
22 miles. The rather large variance is due to wide ranges in operating
speeds of the flushers.

The number of shifts that are operated varies considerably among
cities. Small communities usually are able to do the required cleaning in a single shift. Most of the larger cities, on the other hand,
operate two shifts, and New York City has three shifts daily. New
York City also has used chlorinated sea water during water shortages.

As in other kinds of cleaning, the work should be done when
traffic is lightest. Parked vehicles do not significantly interfere
with flushing, although a better job is done when there are but few
cars standing at the curbs.

Flushers are particularly effective when the pavements are wet
during and after rains. The rain softens the dirt, and the flushing
water moves it away more easily. Substantially less water is required
when pavements are wet, and the flushers can travel faster without
decreasing their effectiveness. However, since the average citizen
is not aware of these advantages, care should be exercised lest the
impression be given that the city is watering the lawn while it is
raining.

Flushers should not be used in freezing weather or when the
temperature is near the freezing point. They may cause icy surfaces
to form, thereby increasing the chances of traffic accidents. Therefore, water should never be used on pavements unless it is certain
that it can evaporate or run off before it freezes.

17.   Based on the information in the above passage, it is   17. ___
       reasonable to assume that the MAIN reason for using water
       under pressure in machine flushing is to
           A. prevent wasting of water during shortages
           B. move the dirt to the curb
           C. make sure that the street is thoroughly wet
           D. clear the dirt that is at the curb

18. Based on the information in the above passage, a flusher   18.___
    that cleans 72 miles of street during a 16-hour period
    is operating at a rate _____ average.
      A. well above the   B. exactly
      C. slightly less than   D. well below the

19. According to the above passage, if there are a few cars   19.___
    standing at the curb when machine flushing is being done,
    the cleaning job
      A. can still be done adequately
      B. will be as effective as when there are many cars
         parked at the curb
      C. will be better than if there are no cars parked at
         the curb
      D. will be done poorly

20. Based on the information in the above passage, which one   20.___
    of the following is the MOST probable reason why New York
    City has three shifts daily for machine flushing operations?
      A. There is more personnel available for use in New
         York City.
      B. New York City has more water available than other
         cities.
      C. New York City's budget allows more money for flushing
         operations.
      D. All the necessary cleaning can't be done with fewer
         shifts.

21. According to the above passage, the flushing of streets   21.___
    during rain may
      A. take longer than street flushing in dry weather
      B. look like a poor practice to the public
      C. decrease the effectiveness of flushing operations
      D. cause a substantial waste of water

22. In the above passage, which of the following is NOT   22.___
    offered as an advantage of flushing streets when they
    are wet?
      A. Street dirt more pliable
      B. Street dirt easier to move
      C. Flusher can move faster
      D. Fewer pedestrians and traffic

23. As used in the above passage, the phrase *watering the*   23.___
    lawn while it is raining means to imply that the city is
      A. trying to impress the public
      B. not aware of the opinions of the average citizen
      C. giving its lawns too much water
      D. doing something unnecessary

24. According to the above passage, flushers should NOT be   24.___
    used in freezing weather because
      A. the water may freeze inside the flushers
      B. slippery driving conditions may be created

C. evaporation or run off of the water from the pavement is likely

D. flushers can't move on icy surfaces

25. During one winter, there were 29 snowfalls with a total snow accumulation for the season of 57.6 inches. The next winter, there were 15 snowfalls with a total snow accumulation for the season of 7.9 inches.
The average snow accumulation per snowfall for the two winters combined was MOST NEARLY _____ inch(es).
   A. 1.00   B. 1.25   C. 1.50   D. 1.75   25._____

26. In District A, 1/6 of the sanitation work force took all its vacation in June, 1/3 of the force took all its vacation in July, and 1/4 took all its vacation in August. What part of the total sanitation work force of the district does this represent?
   A. 3/4   B. 7/12   C. 2/5   D. 3/13   26._____

27. In a four-year period, the Department of Sanitation used 314,997 tons of salt for snow removal. The first year, 79,651 tons were used. The second year, the Department used 6,592 tons less than the first year. In the third year, 11,981 tons of salt more were used than were used in the second year.
The number of tons of salt used in the fourth year was MOST NEARLY
   A. 77,275   B. 77,250   C. 77,225   D. 77,200   27._____

28. Suppose that the number of occupancies that the Department of Sanitation collects from in 6 different sections of the city are, respectively, 1837, 962, 12105, 4923, 26702, and 3819.
The total number of occupancies that the Department must collect from in these 6 sections is MOST NEARLY
   A. 50,355   B. 50,350   C. 50,345   D. 50,340   28._____

29. A rectangular box measures 6 feet by 2½ feet.
If the box is 3 feet deep, the cubic volume of the box is MOST NEARLY _____ cu. inches.
   A. 78,000   B. 41,000   C. 4,500   D. 138   29._____

Questions 30-35.

DIRECTIONS: Questions 30 through 35 are to be answered SOLELY on the basis of the information given in the following passage.

There is no other service offered by a community in which there is such intimate contact with the individual citizen as in the refuse collection service. Because of this intimate contact, it is vitally important that each sanitation man in the service have the proper public relations attitude.

He should be imbued with a genuine desire to provide good service. This service should be impartial, performed in a neat and efficient manner, and the employee should be competent, willing, and efficient.

Every employee in the refuse collection service should be trained in contacting the public whether his job calls for contact in person, by telephone, or by letter. All requests for information and all complaints should be acknowledged promptly and courteously. If practicable, a personal contact should then be made. Later, if necessary, this should be followed up by a proper written reply. Decisions should be backed by the logic of operational problems rather than by flat recitals of codes, ordinances, or rules. But more important than the settling of complaints is the carrying out of the work in such a manner as to eliminate the causes of complaints in the beginning. The chief causes of complaints are the rough handling of containers, spillage of refuse, damage to lawns and shrubbery by collectors, and incomplete removal service. These complaints can be minimized by the training of personnel and by instilling in them a desire to do a good job. The training of drivers to operate their equipment properly is also important. The impression which city equipment makes on the citizen depends on its use as well as on its appearance. A reckless driver or an inconsiderate driver is not liked under any circumstance; but if he is driving a municipal vehicle, his offense is doubly magnified. A driver training program will pay dividends not only in improved public relations but in reduced costs.

30. According to the above passage, the MAIN reason why it is   30.___
    important for a sanitation man to have a good public
    relations attitude is that
        A. refuse collection affects the community's health
        B. his work will be improved
        C. he is in close touch with the private citizen
        D. he is offering an important community service

31. According to the above passage, after a complaint about   31.___
    the refuse collection service is acknowledged, it is
    desirable NEXT to
        A. make an investigation
        B. make a decision about the complaint
        C. interview the complainant in person
        D. follow up with a letter

32. According to the above passage, if a sanitation man has   32.___
    to make a decision in answer to a complaint from a citizen,
    it would be BEST for him to explain to the complainant
        A. why refuse collection operations make this decision
           necessary
        B. the reason for the decision by referring to the
           appropriate rules
        C. the local code which justifies the decision
        D. how the cause of the complaint might have been
           eliminated in the beginning

33. Based on the above passage, it is reasonable to assume   33.___
    that when a sanitation man is assigned to handle requests
    for information or complaints about the refuse collec-
    tion service, he should
    A. give first attention to complaints
    B. give first attention to requests for information
    C. handle both complaints and information requests
       quickly
    D. handle first whatever he has the greatest number of

34. According to the above passage, the one of the following   34.___
    which does NOT seem to be a main source of complaints by
    the public about the refuse collection service is
    A. some material put out for collection being left over
    B. noise of collectors
    C. dirtying of the collection area
    D. damage to property

35. According to the above passage, the public's reaction   35.___
    to a poor driver is
    A. the same no matter what vehicle he is driving
    B. more severe if the vehicle involved is in poor
       condition
    C. more severe if he turns out to be a municipal employee
    D. more severe if he is operating city equipment

Questions 36-40.

DIRECTIONS: Questions 36 through 40 are to be answered SOLELY on
              the basis of the information given in the following
              table.

LOCATION OF FREQUENTLY USED SANITATION EQUIPMENT

Borough	No. of Flushers	No. of Machine Sweepers	No. of Collection Trucks	No. of Snow Plows	No. of Snow Loaders	No. of Sand and Salt Spreaders
Manhattan	112	142	607	487	119	54
Bronx	65	99	422	501	94	97
Brooklyn	132	142	421	542	111	116
Queens	68	107	362	487	82	81
Richmond	36	68	117	164	29	65
Total	413	558	1,929	2,181	435	413

36. Of the total number of snow loaders, the percent located   36.___
    in Manhattan is MOST NEARLY
       A. 29%   B. 28%   C. 27%   D. 26%

37. According to the above table, there are two boroughs that   37.___
    have the same number of
       A. collection trucks   B. flushers
       C. sand and salt spreaders   D. snow plows

38. According to the above table, Richmond does NOT have the 38.___
    smallest number of
    A. snow plows   B. sand and salt spreaders
    C. machine sweepers   D. collection trucks

39. According to the above table, the boroughs that combined 39.___
    have more than one-half the total number of collection
    trucks are
    A. Manhattan and Queens
    B. Bronx and Brooklyn
    C. Bronx, Queens, and Richmond
    D. Brooklyn, Queens, and Richmond

40. By population, four boroughs rank in order from highest 40.___
    to lowest as follows: Brooklyn, Queens, Bronx, Richmond.
    Suppose it is desired that the number of pieces of each
    type of equipment located in these boroughs be in the
    same order as their population.
    Then, according to the above table, the borough or boroughs
    in which this is already the case is
    A. Bronx and Queens   B. Brooklyn and Richmond
    C. Queens *only*   D. Richmond *only*

41. The MAJORITY of home accidents result from 41.___
    A. burns   B. suffocation
    C. falls   D. poisons

42. Of the following, the one that is NOT a symptom of shock 42.___
    is
    A. flushed face   B. weak pulse
    C. cold, clammy skin   D. feeling of weakness

43. In the case of a sprained ankle, an INCORRECT procedure 43.___
    in first aid would be to
    A. elevate the sprained part
    B. apply cold applications
    C. apply a temporary support
    D. massage the part to restore circulation

44. The INCORRECT procedure in treating nosebleeds is to 44.___
    A. have the victim lie down immediately
    B. apply a large, cold, wet cloth to the nose
    C. pack the nose gently with gauze
    D. press the nostrils firmly together

45. In one minute, the heart of a normal man who is resting 45.___
    beats APPROXIMATELY _____ times.
    A. 30   B. 72   C. 98   D. 112

46. All of the following first aid rules for simple nosebleed 46.___
    are approved EXCEPT
    A. gently pinching the nostrils together
    B. applying cold compresses to the nose
    C. blowing the nose gently after bleeding stops to remove
       blood clots
    D. inserting a plug of absorbent cotton

47. In the Holger-Nielsen method of artificial respiration,   47.___
the victim is placed
    A. on his stomach   B. on his back
    C. in a kneeling position   D. in any comfortable position

48. Frequent deaths are reported as a result of running an   48.___
automobile engine in a closed garage.
Death results from
    A. suffocation
    B. carbon monoxide poisoning
    C. excessive humidity
    D. an excess of carbon dioxide in the air

49. Fever, chills, inflamed eyelids, running nose and cough   49.___
are symptoms of
    A. measles   B. chicken pox
    C. tuberculosis   D. scarlet fever

50. Among the usual first signs of measles are listlessness,   50.___
red watery eyes that are sensitive to light, a moderate
fever, and
    A. a running nose   B. a blotchy red rash
    C. a running ear   D. convulsions

KEY (CORRECT ANSWERS)

1. A	11. C	21. B	31. C	41. C
2. B	12. B	22. D	32. A	42. A
3. B	13. A	23. D	33. C	43. D
4. A	14. A	24. B	34. B	44. A
5. A	15. C	25. C	35. D	45. B
6. C	16. D	26. A	36. C	46. C
7. A	17. B	27. B	37. D	47. A
8. D	18. A	28. B	38. B	48. B
9. B	19. A	29. A	39. A	49. A
10. C	20. D	30. C	40. D	50. A

EXAMINATION SECTION

TEST 1

DIRECTIONS: Each question consists of a statement. You are to indicate whether the statement is TRUE (T) or FALSE (F). *PRINT THE LETTER OF THE CORRECT ANSWER IN THE SPACE AT THE RIGHT.*

1. While it may be good for any sanitation man to have a sense of humor, sanitation men should not indulge in jostling or horseplay during duty hours.   1.____

2. One reason why close cooperation among a group of sanitation men engaged in performing a sanitation operation is desirable is that such cooperation usually increases efficiency.   2.____

3. A sanitation man should hold opinions on general matters which agree with those of his supervisor in order to get along with him.   3.____

4. A Department of Sanitation collection crew has the responsibility of acting in such a way as to maintain favorable public opinion.   4.____

5. If a sanitation man does not clearly understand any aspect of a foreman's order, he should first ask for clarification of the order before carrying it out.   5.____

6. On a hot summer day, it would be perfectly proper for a sanitation man to leave his route for a few minutes for a glass of beer so that he could continue his work refreshed.   6.____

7. If a sanitation loader's partner suddenly starts to avoid lifting the heavier cans, the loader should try to determine whether his partner has some difficulty such as an injury which prevents him from lifting in his usual manner.   7.____

8. A sanitation man who sees a man throw a smoking mattress out of a window on to the sidewalk should arrest the man for dumping rubbish on the sidewalk.   8.____

9. A sanitation man who sees that the limb of a tree is hiding a *No Parking* sign on a street where alternate side of the street parking is in effect should cut the limb down right away.   9.____

10. A good idea at Christmas time is for the sanitation men in a district to pick out one man to visit the residents of the district in order to give them the season's greetings and accept whatever gifts they may offer.   10.____

11. Disagreement with the wisdom of an order of a superior is not sufficient grounds for refusal to obey the order by a sanitation man.

11.____

12. If a sanitation man, while loading late at night, finds a pistol in the top of a garbage can, he should question the residents of the area to find out if anything is wrong.

12.____

13. A sanitation crew should see to it that a collection truck is always partly full so as to deaden the rattling caused by the movement of an empty truck.

13.____

14. The main reason for alternate side of the street parking regulations is to make it easier for the Department of Sanitation to do its job of cleaning the streets.

14.____

15. Congested business areas with heavy pedestrian traffic would generally require more frequent sweeping by the Department of Sanitation than residential areas.

15.____

16. A violation of the Sanitary Code in a new residential district is not any less serious than the same violation in an old, congested district.

16.____

17. Sanitation Department litter baskets are placed on the streets of business districts so that nearby storekeepers will have a place to put their business waste.

17.____

18. An important advantage of using steel scows instead of wooden scows for carrying waste from the city is that steel scows are more fireproof.

18.____

19. A properly designed Sanitary Code helps to insure the success of a community sanitation program.

19.____

20. It is generally best for the collection route of a sanitation truck to start from a point in the sanitation district which is near the disposal site for the refuse and to end at a remote edge of the district.

20.____

21. If two sanitation men who are assigned to do a job together cannot agree on how to do the work, the best way to solve this problem is for the two men to have as little to do with each other as possible.

21.____

22. The activities of the Department of Sanitation can affect the incidence of disease even though the Department of Health has the main job of controlling the disease.

22.____

Questions 23-26.

DIRECTIONS: Questions 23 through 26 are to be answered TRUE (T) or
               FALSE (F) on the basis of the information contained in
               the following paragraph.

The number of containers picked up per mile is a better index of
the labor requirements for the pick-up operation than the number of
houses served per mile. The labor time needed to collect refuse over
a given distance increases in direct proportion to the number of
containers which must be lifted. It has been found that the number
of houses serviced per mile is quite adequate as an index of labor
requirements in those cities where the garbage and domestic refuse
is deposited in a single standard container and the practice is
enforced by law, but in such cases the number of houses serviced is
equal to the number of containers picked up.

23.   The greater the number of containers of refuse which must   23.____
       be lifted within a given distance travelled, the greater
       the labor time required to collect the refuse over the
       distance.

24.   The number of houses serviced per mile sometimes equals   24.____
       the number of containers picked up per mile by the collec-
       tor.

25.   The number of houses serviced per mile is not an adequate   25.____
       index of the labor requirements for the pick-up operation
       in any city.

26.   In those cities where the practice of depositing garbage   26.____
       and domestic refuse in separate standard containers is
       enforced by law, the number of houses serviced per mile
       is a good index of labor requirements.

Questions 27-32.

DIRECTIONS: Questions 27 through 32 are to be answered TRUE (T) or
               FALSE (F) on the basis of the information contained in
               the following paragraph.

Those unplanned and undesirable occurrences which injure people,
destroy equipment and materials, interrupt the orderly progress of
any activity, or waste time and money are called accidents. Some
degree of hazard is associated with every form of activity, and
every uncontrolled hazard will, in time, produce its share of
accidents. Accidents do not just happen. They are caused by unsafe
conditions or unsafe acts or both. A safety program is an organized
effort to eliminate physical hazards and unsafe practices in order
to prevent accidents and their resultant injuries. Safety is not
something to be thought of only when no other duties are pressing,
but must become part of every activity of every day.

27. A happening that is not wanted and not planned and wastes time and money is called an accident.   27._____

28. There is no activity that is free of hazard.   28._____

29. Hazardous conditions are uncontrollable.   29._____

30. An accident will not happen if the physical conditions are safe.   30._____

31. A safety program seeks to prevent accidents by getting rid of unsafe practices and physical hazards.   31._____

32. Safety is apart from every day activities.   32._____

Questions 33-36.

DIRECTIONS: Questions 33 through 36 are to be answered TRUE (T) or FALSE (F) on the basis of the information contained in the following paragraph.

Standardizing the size of a satisfactory refuse container may determine how often refuse is collected. A standard size is arrived at by considering the ease of handling the can and the average rate of accumulation of the refuse at the household. An excessive amount of refuse at the household should be avoided as it invariably leads to inferior sanitation practices.

33. The frequency of refuse collection may be influenced by the size of the refuse container.   33._____

34. Ease of handling a refuse can is a factor in arriving at a standard size for a refuse container.   34._____

35. The cause of poorer sanitation practices is invariably excessive piling up of refuse at the household.   35._____

36. Excessive production of refuse at the household should be prevented.   36._____

Questions 37-40.

DIRECTIONS: Questions 37 through 40 are to be answered TRUE (T) or FALSE (F) on the basis of the information contained in the following paragraph.

In a comparison made between collection by means of open-body trucks and collection by means of mechanical packers, it was found that refuse collectors working with mechanical compaction trucks spent approximately seven percent of the pick-up time in waiting. Only two percent of the pick-up time was consumed by collectors in waiting in the case of collection by open-body trucks.

37. In the comparison made, more than one type of truck was used.   37.___

38. A mechanical compaction truck travels more slowly than an open-body truck.   38.___

39. A comparison indicates that collectors spend a smaller percentage of pick-up time in waiting when they work with open-body trucks than when they work with mechanical compaction trucks.   39.___

40. In refuse collection, the type of truck used is a factor influencing time spent on one element of the operation.   40.___

Questions 41-46.

DIRECTIONS: Questions 41 through 46 are to be answered TRUE (T) or FALSE (F) on the basis of the information contained in the following paragraph.

It is possible for an inspection program of sanitation equipment to contribute toward the maximum utilization of equipment only if the inspections are properly scheduled, performed, and acted upon. This is so because the maximum utilization of equipment depends on a number of factors. A long life span for the equipment must be obtained by proper maintenance and repair. Organization and scheduling the manpower and equipment must be directed toward preventing the equipment from remaining unnecessarily idle. The maximum period of time for the use of any piece of motor equipment is that interval between the instant the equipment is received and the moment it becomes obsolete, the interval of availability. The purpose of an inspection program is to help expand the volume of work accomplished by equipment within the interval of availability, which in modern times is rapidly contracting.

41. If inspections of sanitation equipment are properly scheduled, performed, and acted upon, they insure maximum utilization of equipment.   41.___

42. To get a long life span for the equipment, proper maintenance and repair are necessary.   42.___

43. Maximum use of manpower is obtained when there is maximum use of equipment.   43.___

44. The longest period of time possible for the use of a piece of motor equipment is the time between the moment it becomes obsolete and the instant it is received.   44.___

45. The purpose of an equipment inspection program is to help increase the volume of work produced by the equipment from the time the equipment is received until the time it becomes obsolete.   45.___

46. In modern times, the maximum period of time for the use   46.____
of any piece of motor equipment is rapidly shrinking.

Questions 47-49.

DIRECTIONS: Questions 47 through 49 are to be answered TRUE (T) or FALSE (F) on the basis of the information contained in the following paragraph.

    When in use, the storage battery becomes hot, and water evaporates from the cells of the battery; so clean water, preferably distilled, must be added at frequent intervals. This action keeps the level of the battery liquid above the top of the battery plates.

47. All water loss from a storage battery occurs when the   47.____
battery is in use.

48. The water added to a storage battery does not have to be   48.____
distilled.

49. Water in the storage battery must be kept level with the   49.____
top of the battery plates.

50. An operator who drives at 37 miles per hour in a 35 mile   50.____
per hour speed zone is, for all practical purposes, driving within the legal speed limit.

KEY (CORRECT ANSWERS)

1. T	11. T	21. F	31. T	41. F
2. T	12. F	22. T	32. F	42. T
3. F	13. F	23. T	33. T	43. F
4. T	14. T	24. T	34. T	44. T
5. T	15. T	25. F	35. F	45. T
6. F	16. T	26. F	36. F	46. T
7. T	17. F	27. T	37. T	47. F
8. F	18. T	28. T	38. F	48. T
9. F	19. T	29. F	39. T	49. F
10. F	20. F	30. F	40. T	50. F

TEST 2

DIRECTIONS: Each question consists of a statement. You are to indicate whether the statement is TRUE (T) or FALSE (F). *PRINT THE LETTER OF THE CORRECT ANSWER IN THE SPACE AT THE RIGHT.*

1. Since the law provides that a pedestrian must yield the right-of-way to vehicles proceeding directly ahead on a green light, a good driver, in order to prevent traffic delays, should blow his horn and exercise his legal rights when a pedestrian attempts to cross in front of him in such a situation.

    1.___

2. If three cars going north, south, and east, respectively, arrive at an unmarked intersection at the same time, and the standard rule is that the car to the driver's right has the right-of-way, then the car going north has the right-of-way.

    2.___

3. When parking a car uphill, the rear wheels should be turned so that the rear of the vehicle will coast into the curb if the brakes should fail.

    3.___

4. In order to steer out of a skid where the rear end is swinging toward the left, the driver should steer to the left.

    4.___

5. In the city, a driver who extends his left arm at a 45° angle above the horizontal is giving the legal hand signal for a right turn.

    5.___

6. A sanitation driver who discovers that the engine of his truck has become overheated because the water in the cooling system has been emptied through a small leak in the bottom of the radiator should quickly fill the cooling system with cold water.

    6.___

7. Road traffic signs bearing the same type of message are made in a standard shape mainly for economy in manufacture.

    7.___

8. On roads in this state, a diamond-shaped yellow sign indicates a hazardous condition which requires a reduction in speed.

    8.___

9. The generator connected to the gasoline engine of a truck converts mechanical energy into electrical energy to be used in the operation of the truck.

    9.___

10. If a driver, who has been traveling north on a two-way street, starts to make a correct right turn into another two-way street, which crosses the north and south bound street at right angles, and his truck stalls when it is halfway through the turn, the truck is now in the path of traffic lanes directed east and south.

    10.___

11. A safety-conscious truck operator should check the instruments on the dashboard before turning on the ignition of his truck.   11.___

12. Proper lubrication is extremely important for the efficient operation of a gasoline engine.   12.___

13. If a car with standard shift is standing still with its engine running, and the clutch pedal is pushed down, the engine will stop opening until the driver shifts into gear.   13.___

14. An important difference between a diesel engine and a gasoline engine is the type of fuel used.   14.___

15. A broken or slipping fan belt cannot cause an automobile engine to overheat.   15.___

16. One effect of the action of a piston in a gasoline engine is to expel the gaseous wastes of combustion from the cylinder within which the piston travels.   16.___

17. A solid line used in conjunction with a broken line in the center of a highway means that the driver on the broken line side may cross if the way is clear.   17.___

18. As the car ahead increases its speed, the minimum distance permissible for safety between the car ahead and a car directly behind increases even though the brakes of the two cars may have equal stopping distances.   18.___

19. The distributor connected to the gasoline engine of a truck takes the fuel to each cylinder of the engine.   19.___

20. If a car coming from the opposite direction at night does not lower its lights in response to the dimming of a sanitation truck's lights, the sanitation driver should put his high beam back on to counteract the glare.   20.___

21. *Ashes are transported from Department of Sanitation incinerators to points of ultimate disposal.*
In this sentence, the word *ultimate* means NEARLY the same as *final*.   21.___

22. *In some areas where mechanical sweepers are used, supplementary manual cleaning is required.*
In this sentence, the word *supplementary* means NEARLY the same as *additional*.   22.___

23. *It was stipulated that ferrous metals should be used.*
In this sentence, the word *stipulated* means NEARLY the same as *agreed*.   23.___

24. *We find a different type of residue here.*
    In this sentence, the word *residue* means NEARLY the same as *inhabitant.*

24.___

25. *Several giant segments lay there.*
    In this sentence, the word *segments* means NEARLY the same as *parts.*

25.___

26. *The number of usable fill properties continues to dwindle.*
    In this sentence, the word *dwindle* means NEARLY the same as *multiply.*

26.___

27. *The salient provisions were given.*
    In this sentence, the word *salient* means NEARLY the same as *prominent.*

27.___

28. *Rate of putrefaction must be considered.*
    In this sentence, the word *putrefaction* means NEARLY the same as *rotting.*

28.___

29. *The increase in the number of accidents is negligible.*
    In this sentence, the word *negligible* means NEARLY the same as *serious.*

29.___

30. *He received monetary assistance.*
    In this sentence, the word *monetary* means NEARLY the same as *temporary.*

30.___

31. *Litigation delayed construction of the new incinerator.*
    In this sentence, the word *litigation* means NEARLY the same as *rising costs.*

31.___

32. *Proximity of the site is important.*
    In this sentence, the word *proximity* means NEARLY the same as *closeness.*

32.___

33. *At sanitary landfills, refuse is not dumped indiscriminately.*
    In this sentence, the word *indiscriminately* means NEARLY the same as *before burning.*

33.___

34. *Improvised equipment is seldom used.*
    In this sentence, the word *improvised* means NEARLY the same as *worn out.*

34.___

35. *At marine loading stations, refuse barges are loaded by gravity.*
    In this sentence, the word *gravity* means NEARLY the same as *shovel.*

35.___

36. *Many difficulties were encountered in the operation.*
    In this sentence, the word *encountered* means NEARLY the same as *met.*

36.___

37. *Traffic control facilitates the collection of waste in a large city.*
In this sentence, the word *facilitates* means NEARLY the same as *eases*.

37.___

38. *Four persons were extricated immediately.*
In this sentence, the word *extricated* means NEARLY the same as *treated*.

38.___

39. *Large objects produce extensive damage to mechanical equipment of furnaces.*
In this sentence, the word *extensive* means NEARLY the same as *slight*.

39.___

40. *The car's headlights flickered on the dark street.*
In this sentence, the word *flickered* means NEARLY the same as *shone brightly*.

40.___

41. *The sweeper was retained when the vacuum cleaners were installed.*
In this sentence, the word *retained* means NEARLY the same as *kept*.

41.___

42. *Several men had dismantled the engine.*
In this sentence, the word *dismantled* means NEARLY the same as *inspected*.

42.___

43. *The switch should be pushed down when the car approaches.*
In this sentence, the word *approaches* means NEARLY the same as *comes near*.

43.___

44. *There is a possibility of ground water contamination.*
In this sentence, the word *contamination* means NEARLY the same as *radioactivity*.

44.___

45. *The components of refuse must be segregated.*
In this sentence, the word *components* means NEARLY the same as *containers*.

45.___

46. *The arrival of the tractor coincided with that of the dump truck.*
In this sentence, the word *coincided* means NEARLY the same as *interfered*.

46.___

47. *Every idea sent to the Employee Suggestion Program is appraised.*
In this sentence, the word *appraised* means NEARLY the same as *judged*.

47.___

48. *An adjacent garage maintained snow equipment.*
In this sentence, the word *adjacent* means NEARLY the same as *neighboring*.

48.___

49. *Check all facts before analyzing a report.*
    In this sentence, the word *analyzing* means NEARLY the same as *submitting.*
    49.___

50. *The abatement of odors affects living conditions.*
    In this sentence, the word *abatement* means NEARLY the same as *reduction.*
    50.___

KEY (CORRECT ANSWERS)

1. F	11. F	21. T	31. F	41. T
2. T	12. T	22. T	32. T	42. F
3. F	13. F	23. T	33. F	43. T
4. T	14. T	24. F	34. F	44. F
5. T	15. F	25. T	35. F	45. F
6. F	16. T	26. F	36. T	46. F
7. F	17. T	27. T	37. T	47. T
8. T	18. T	28. T	38. F	48. T
9. T	19. F	29. F	39. F	49. F
10. F	20. F	30. F	40. F	50. T

TEST 3

DIRECTIONS: Each question consists of a statement. You are to
indicate whether the statement is TRUE (T) or FALSE (F).
*PRINT THE LETTER OF THE CORRECT ANSWER IN THE SPACE AT
THE RIGHT.*

1. According to the Sanitary Code, metal receptacles shall   1.___
   not be filled to a greater height than six inches from
   the top thereof.

2. According to the Sanitary Code, metal receptacles, when   2.___
   properly filled, shall not contain more than four cubic
   feet of material.

3. According to the Sanitary Code, it is the duty of every   3.___
   owner or person in charge of a building to provide, or
   cause to be provided, sufficient receptacles made of
   metal for holding, without leakage, all ashes, garbage,
   refuse, and liquid waste substances that may accumulate
   during 72 consecutive hours.

4. It is unlawful for a person other than an employee of   4.___
   the Department of Sanitation to interfere with garbage
   or refuse put out by householders.

5. It is unlawful for any person or public agency to conduct   5.___
   or operate any piece or parcel of land within the city as
   a dump without having first obtained a permit from the
   Commissioner of Sanitation.

6. A sanitation man is subject to penalties if he assists in   6.___
   the collection of trade wastes on his own time with a
   private truck.

7. A sanitation man is subject to penalties if he sorts over   7.___
   materials received for collection or disposal.

8. A sanitation man is subject to penalties if he accepts   8.___
   material distributed by a citizen not authorized by the
   Commissioner of Sanitation.

9. A sanitation man is subject to penalties if he is absent   9.___
   from his post of duty without authority.

10. A sanitation man is subject to penalties if he fails to   10.___
    report improper loads.

11. A carbon tetrachloride extinguisher works by smothering   11.___
    the fire.

12. Hot residue from incinerators may safely be dumped into   12.____
    trucks for transportation to landfills.

13. A carbon dioxide extinguisher puts out fires by cooling   13.____
    them down.

14. A soda acid extinguisher is effective in an electrical   14.____
    fire.

15. The Department of Sanitation services all city depart-   15.____
    ments in the refilling of carbon dioxide fire extin-
    guishers.

16. A sanitation man involved in an accident while driving a   16.____
    Department of Sanitation vehicle must report it to the
    division of safety.

17. Certain types of work make the use of safety equipment,   17.____
    such as life belts, rubber aprons, and wooden shoes, a
    requirement for the men.

18. Once a driver's license is suspended, the Division of   18.____
    Safety must require his dismissal.

19. The Division of Safety may require that a driver be given   19.____
    special driving training if he is involved in an accident
    even though the driver was not to blame.

20. Riding on the fenders or running board of a Department of   20.____
    Sanitation truck is not only unsafe but a violation of
    the Code of Discipline.

21. An unconscious person should be given a liquid stimulant.   21.____

22. A wound is any break in the skin or mucous membrane.   22.____

23. A key rule in first aid is to keep the patient cool.   23.____

24. The first thing to do when treating an unconscious person   24.____
    is to sit him up and give him air.

25. First aid is the assistance given an injured person while   25.____
    waiting for the doctor to arrive.

26. A loaded truck weighs 5,400 pounds. If the truck weighs   26.____
    twice as much as the load, the load weighs 1,800 pounds.

27. If eight men are needed to sweep a particular area in   27.____
    6 hours, it would only take six men to sweep this area
    in 8 hours.

28. If a collection truck travels a half mile in 10 minutes,   28.____
    its speed is 15 miles per hour.

29. If twelve cans of sweepings fill a truck which can hold   29.____
    1½ tons, three cans of sweepings will fill a truck holding
    ½ ton.

30. The capacity of the body of a hired truck which is six   30.____
    feet wide, ten feet long, and six feet high is the same
    as one which measures six feet by twelve feet by five feet.

31. A district officer is selected to act as district snow   31.____
    inspector to assist in the direction and supervision of
    hired equipment, department hauling operations, and
    contract snow removal.

32. Piling of snow is resorted to only when the forecast is   32.____
    for below freezing temperatures and the accumulation of
    snow makes it impossible to dispose of otherwise.

33. An emergency snow laborer who loses a tool is docked a   33.____
    number of hours equivalent to the price of the tool.

34. In scattering snow, the most efficient procedure is to   34.____
    scatter it near corner sewers.

35. If it should snow outside of regular working hours, all   35.____
    sanitation men are to call the central office for orders.

36. A snow plow route is at least ten miles long and may be   36.____
    longer if there is not too much traffic.

37. Well-treated snow equipment needs no special supervision   37.____
    or testing to be ready for a quick start in winter.

38. Plans for snow removal are made long before the snow   38.____
    season starts.

39. The responsibility of the Department of Sanitation for   39.____
    snow removal derives from the city charter.

40. Chamois is a good drying agent after glass has been   40.____
    washed.

41. Carbon tetrachloride is commonly used to soften hardened   41.____
    chewing gum on floors.

42. Fine emery cloth and oil is a good cleaning agent for   42.____
    plated plumbing fixtures.

43. An order for supplies on a storeroom is called a   43.____
    requisition.

44. Goods subject to damage by heat should not be stored   44.____
    near the ceiling if possible.

45. The most efficient method of storekeeping is to order   45.___
    supplies only when the available supply has become
    exhausted.

46. Both sodium fluoride and D.D.T. are insecticides.   46.___

47. Floors of elevators should be mopped daily.   47.___

48. Floor brushes require daily washing in order to be   48.___
    maintained in an acceptably clean condition.

49. Floor brushes which have been worn down in normal use   49.___
    may be used to sweep sidewalks and yard areas.

50. Cleaners should be instructed never to wring out a mop   50.___
    by hand.

_____

KEY (CORRECT ANSWERS)

1. F	11. T	21. F	31. T	41. T
2. F	12. F	22. T	32. T	42. F
3. F	13. F	23. F	33. T	43. T
4. T	14. F	24. F	34. F	44. F
5. T	15. T	25. T	35. F	45. F
6. F	16. T	26. T	36. F	46. T
7. T	17. T	27. T	37. F	47. T
8. F	18. F	28. F	38. T	48. F
9. T	19. F	29. F	39. T	49. T
10. T	20. T	30. T	40. T	50. T

_____

EXAMINATION SECTION

TEST 1

DIRECTIONS: Each question consists of a statement. You are to
indicate whether the statement is TRUE (T) or FALSE (F).
*PRINT THE LETTER OF THE CORRECT ANSWER IN THE SPACE AT
THE RIGHT.*

Questions 1-15.

DIRECTIONS: Questions 1 through 15 are to be answered SOLELY on the
basis of the information contained in the following
passage.

Formerly, all the records on material were kept on a volume basis
(cubic yards), but a few years ago this was changed to the more
accurate weight basis. Since we do not have scales at all locations,
approximate weights have been set for different types of vehicles
with allowance being made for the difference between summer and
winter material. Sanitation men must be familiar with these established weights since they are used daily in converting yardage load
figures to conform to the present requirements of our statistics.
In addition, at the incinerators a maximum weight for various vehicles
is set as they indicate an overload of non-combustible material such
as ashes.

Certain city agencies and recognized charitable organizations are
permitted to use dumping facilities without cost, but only if they are
on our approved list and their own vehicles are used. Examples of
such organizations are the Salvation Army and Catholic Charities.
City agencies, such as the Borough Public Works and the Park Department, likewise are accorded free dumping privileges, but they are
subject to our rules in regard to non-combustible materials. Government and state agencies are required to pay for dumping privileges
the same as anyone else.

The officer at any of our locations has no discretion in regard
to permitting private concerns the privilege of dumping without paying
therefor and without conforming to our regulations.

On very rare occasions, a concern such as a bank may be required
to witness the destruction by burning of certain checks or records.
When this occurs, arrangements have to be made by the concern through
the main office and even then the officer at the location must not
permit them to dispose of the material until after calling the main
office for permission. The procedure applies to each and every load
so disposited, and in all cases an entry of the incident must be
made in the log.

1. Records kept on a volume basis are more accurate than weight records. 1.___

2. The Department of Sanitation has scales at all disposal locations. 2.___

3. Because of the shortage of time, volume records are kept at some locations. 3.___

4. Allowances are made in the approximate weights set for different type vehicles according to the seasons. 4.___

5. A sanitation man can easily convert yardage load figures to weight figures with the knowledge of the established weight for different type vehicles. 5.___

6. A maximum weight is set for various vehicles at incinerators since greater amounts indicate an overload of non-combustible material. 6.___

7. Any charitable agency may have the Department of Sanitation take their refuse to a city dump. 7.___

8. The Salvation Army and similar approved charitable organizations may dump freely at a city dump if they use their own truck. 8.___

9. City agencies have free dumping privileges for combustible materials. 9.___

10. Government and state agencies are exempt from fees for dumping privileges. 10.___

11. An officer at a Department of Sanitation location may, in some cases, grant a private concern special privileges of dumping without payment and without conforming to Department of Sanitation regulations. 11.___

12. Banks or similar concerns may arrange to have witnesses present at the burning of checks or records. 12.___

13. A bank wishing to make arrangements to burn records must first contact the nearest incinerator plant. 13.___

14. Each load which requires a witness must be arranged for independently. 14.___

15. Where arrangements are made to burn records, an entry of the incident must be made in the log. 15.___

16. The Office of Engineering gets many valuable ideas from the Employees' Suggestion System. 16.___

17. The Department of Sanitation is planning to use dark gray   17.___
    and black color schemes on trucks in order to improve
    their appearance.

18. The Office of Engineering makes recommendations to the   18.___
    City Planning Commission concerning street layouts in
    order to simplify waste collection.

19. The Department of Sanitation uses three different makes   19.___
    of mechanical sweepers.

20. High birms are unusually tall snow fences.   20.___

21. Cover can be obtained for a fill adjacent to open water   21.___
    by digging out some nearby upland.

22. A Department of Sanitation permittee must permanently   22.___
    affix the metal plates he receives from the chief clerk
    to each side of his vehicle.

23. The Bureau of Cleaning and Collection is under the super-   23.___
    vision of the Director of Operations.

24. The Director of Administration supervises two major   24.___
    administrative bureaus: the Bureau of Fiscal Service
    and the Bureau of General Service.

25. The Department of Sanitation is divided into two basic   25.___
    branches: Operation and Administration.

26. Truck permits for private waste conveyances are issued   26.___
    as a form of regulatory control and also since they add
    a source of revenue.

27. Picking or reclamation privileges are awarded annually   27.___
    to the highest bidder.

28. More ashes are put out in warm weather than in cold   28.___
    weather.

29. Collections of waste material are heavier toward the   29.___
    latter part of the week.

30. A snowstorm has little effect on the collection of waste   30.___
    material.

31. A panscraper should be used when fine cleaning a street   31.___
    paved with cobblestones.

32. Collection trucks are used to haul residue from incinera-   32.___
    tors to a final disposal plant.

33. Nelson loaders are used to load garbage into compactor trucks.   33.__

34. Bleeding poles are used to make a fewer run faster.   34.__

35. Solar cans are used to hold office refuse in a section office.   35.__

36. Crossbars are used to carry garbage cans.   36.__

37. Push brooms are used for hand sweeping.   37.__

38. Hand sweeping is more efficient at removing street dust than hand flushing.   38.__

39. A mechanical sweeper can only sweep as much area as an efficient hand sweeper.   39.__

40. Flushing operations are best when vehicular traffic is at a minimum.   40.__

41. Refuse which is used at landfills is untreated and merely covered over with ashes.   41.__

42. Drivers of sanitation trucks do not need to record loads brought to a marine loading station.   42.__

43. The Bureau of Waste Disposal is divided into three divisions which operate destructors, marine operations, and landfills.   43.__

44. There are two types of marine loading stations, the open and the covered.   44.__

45. The purpose of a motorized litter patrol is the emptying of litter baskets in areas where there is much pedestrian traffic.   45.__

46. The extension of one-side-of-the-street parking has not helped the Department of Sanitation program for mechanical curb sweeping because of the chronic violations.   46.__

47. More than half the city now receives daily collection service.   47.__

48. The Department of Sanitation uses incineration as the basic method of waste disposal.   48.__

49. For purposes of street cleaning and waste collection, the Department of Sanitation has divided the city into 150 sections.

50. The City Charter provides that the Commissioner of Sanita-   50.___
     tion shall have charge and control of sweeping, cleaning,
     sprinkling, flushing, and washing of the streets except
     streets in the boroughs of Queens and Richmond not having
     permanent pavement.

———

KEY (CORRECT ANSWERS)

1. F	11. F	21. F	31. F	41. F
2. F	12. T	22. T	32. T	42. F
3. F	13. F	23. T	33. F	43. T
4. T	14. T	24. T	34. T	44. T
5. T	15. T	25. F	35. F	45. T
6. T	16. T	26. T	36. F	46. F
7. F	17. F	27. T	37. T	47. T
8. T	18. F	28. F	38. F	48. F
9. T	19. T	29. F	39. F	49. F
10. F	20. F	30. F	40. T	50. T

———

TEST 2

DIRECTIONS: Each question consists of a statement. You are to indicate whether the statement is TRUE (T) or FALSE (F). *PRINT THE LETTER OF THE CORRECT ANSWER IN THE SPACE AT THE RIGHT.*

Questions 1-15.

DIRECTIONS: Questions 1 through 15 are to be answered SOLELY on the basis of the information given in the following passage.

New York City, the hub of industrial and financial activities and the home of 8,000,000 inhabitants, maintains a foremost position by the attention it gives to the removal of snow and ice from city street The importance of this task can be appreciated if we consider the catastrophe that would result if a snowstorm were inadequately combatted: Traffic would be paralyzed; food and fuel shipments hindered; fire trucks, ambulances, and other emergency vehicles seriously impeded; transportation generally hampered. Small wonder, then, that the function of snow removal is clearly mandated to the Department of Sanitation by Paragraph 755 of the City Charter. The Department's operational standards, skilled personnel, and special equipment are designed to cope with this seasonal emergency.

To combat a snowstorm effectively from its start, our Department uses a variety of equipment. Each phase of the storm calls for the use of special equipment. The beginning of a storm, depending upon its anticipated intensity, usually brings into operation rotary brooms and sand and salt spreaders. As the storm increases, the plow equipment gains in importance. Each following activity, such as sewering, piling, and flushing, calls for a special type of equipment which, by its proper and timely use, marks the difference between success and failure.

The best conceived plan and the most adequate equipment are useless without the personnel capable of putting the plan into effect.

For that reason, conscientious and skilled employees are chosen and trained as field instructors through whom other employees are taught the effective use and care of equipment.

It remains for the field instructor to develop the students' skill as operators of snow equipment and to impress the importance of applying that skill effectively in snow removal operations.

1. New York City has eight million inhabitants.   1.__

2. New York City's attention to the removal of snow and ice   2.__
    from the streets has no effect on its foremost position.

3. If snow were not removed after a snowstorm, traffic would   3.___
   be paralyzed.

4. A snowstorm has little effect on food and fuel shipments.   4.___

5. Snow removal is mandated to the Department of Sanitation   5.___
   by the City Charter.

6. The Department has special equipment designed to cope with   6.___
   this seasonal emergency.

7. To fight a snowstorm, the City needs little variety of   7.___
   equipment.

8. During each part of a storm, special equipment is called   8.___
   into use as needed.

9. The start of a storm brings out rotary brooms and sand   9.___
   and salt spreaders.

10. If a storm increases, plows are used.   10.___

11. With a good plan and good equipment, one can put the   11.___
    plan into effect without capable personnel.

12. Conscientious and skilled employees are chosen and trained   12.___
    as field inspectors.

13. Other employees are taught the effective use of equipment   13.___
    by the field instructors.

14. The field instructors should not develop their students'   14.___
    skills as operators of snow equipment.

15. An instructor should impress the student with the need   15.___
    to apply his skill in effectively using equipment to
    remove snow.

Questions 16-25.

DIRECTIONS: The following lists some of the equipment required for
             street operations. A brief description of the use of
             each article is noted. Questions 16 through 25 are to
             be answered by using the information below. You are to
             decide whether the statement is TRUE (T) or FALSE (F).

    Push brooms .... Hand sweeping
    Panscraper .... Rough cleaning
    Can carrier .... Conveying cans of street dirt
    Shovel .... Picking up street dirt
    Hose reel .... Convey hose
    Nozzle .... Regulate water flow
    Pick .... For ice conditions
    Hydrant pump .... Pump water from hydrant barrel

```
Red flags and lanterns ...... Signal of danger
Wire baskets ............... Pedestrians litter
Solar cans ................. Pedestrians litter
Can shed ................... Storage of dirt cans
```

16. A panscraper is used for fine cleaning.   16.__

17. A hose reel is used to carry hose.   17.__

18. A can carrier is used to carry cans of street dirt.   18.__

19. A push broom is used to sweep curbs mechanically.   19.__

20. A shovel is used to pick up snow.   20.__

21. A hose is used to wash streets.   21.__

22. A pick is used to pick up street dirt.   22.__

23. A nozzle is used to connect hose to a hydrant.   23.__

24. Red flags and lantern are danger signals.   24.__

25. Wire baskets and solar cans are used for the same purpose.   25.__

26. You should get help before lifting a large or heavy object   26.__
    which you believe is beyond your strength.

27. In lifting a heavy object, keep your feet together and   27.__
    never crouch down.

28. A person who is unconscious can be restored to conscious-   28.__
    ness by giving him an alcoholic stimulant.

29. Heat exhaustion is the same as sunstroke.   29.__

30. A general rule for treating a person seriously hurt is   30.__
    to keep him lying down.

31. Immediate attention should be given to a fracture even   31.__
    before serious bleeding which is occurring at the same
    time.

32. The chief dangers of wounds are severe bleeding, infection, 32.__
    and shock.

33. A first aider should make no attempt to clean a wound;   33.__
    that should be left for the doctor.

34. Whenever there is severe injury, shock is likely to occur.   34.__

35. Where a person is suffering from poisoning, a good remedy   35.__
    is to give an anesthetic.

Questions 36-45.

DIRECTIONS: Questions 36 through 45 are to be answered on the basis
               of the material contained in the following passage.

About 800 supervisors of all grades have been indoctrinated in
corrective methods for unsafe practices and conditions. These
instructions help to prevent accidental injuries to the men in their
charge. New employees, as a part of their instruction at the
Training Center, are given an outline of the safety work and the
accident prevention operations of the Department by an officer of
this division.

An essential part of this work is the reporting of all personal
injuries involving loss of time of one or more working days. As an
indication of the success of this work, it can be shown that during
1969 there was a decrease under 1968 of 14.2% in the number of
employee injuries causing loss of one day or more.

36.   There are 900 supervisors who help prevent accidental   36.___
       injuries to the men in their charge.

37.   The supervisors have been taught how to correct unsafe   37.___
       practices and conditions.

38.   The instructions in safety are of no help in preventing   38.___
       accidents.

39.   New employees are given safety instruction at the Training   39.___
       Center.

40.   It is necessary to report only injuries involving loss of   40.___
       more than five days of working time.

41.   It is necessary to report only injuries involving loss of   41.___
       property.

42.   Reporting any injuries is not essential to constructive   42.___
       safety work.

43.   The success of this accident prevention work can be shown   43.___
       by the decrease in employee injuries.

44.   In 1968, there were 14.2% less employee injuries than in   44.___
       1969.

45.   The injuries referred to are those causing the loss of   45.___
       one day or more.

46.   The sum of 2345 and 4483 is 6882.   46.___

47.   One-fifth of 295 is 59.   47.___

48.   The difference between 2876 and 1453 is 1423.   48. __

49.   If each of 5 sections has 15 solar cans, the total of   49. __
all five sections is 75 cans.

50.   If there are 245 sections in the city, the average number   50. __
of sections for each of the 5 counties is 49 sections.

————

KEY (CORRECT ANSWERS)

1. T	11. F	21. T	31. F	41. F
2. F	12. T	22. F	32. T	42. F
3. T	13. T	23. F	33. T	43. T
4. F	14. F	24. T	34. T	44. F
5. T	15. T	25. T	35. F	45. T
6. T	16. F	26. T	36. F	46. F
7. F	17. T	27. F	37. T	47. T
8. T	18. T	28. F	38. F	48. T
9. T	19. F	29. F	39. T	49. T
10. T	20. F	30. T	40. F	50. T

————

TEST 3

DIRECTIONS: Each question consists of a statement. You are to indicate whether the statement is TRUE (T) or FALSE (F). *PRINT THE LETTER OF THE CORRECT ANSWER IN THE SPACE AT THE RIGHT.*

Questions 1-10.

DIRECTIONS: Questions 1 through 10 are to be answered on the basis of the material contained in the following passage.

When a summons is issued in lieu of an arrest for an unlawful act, the Inspector should first make certain of the offender's identity. The summonses are always made returnable to the local District City Civil Court having jurisdiction in the area in which the offense is committed. Inspectors issuing such summons should allow at least a twenty-four hour period to elapse between the time of service and the time for arraignment. At the completion of each Inspector's tour, a card is submitted to the Division Office, describing in detail the violator, his address, the violation, place of occurrence, court, and returnable date.

The summons (or arrest) cards are carefully checked against the Premises File and also against an Alphabetical File for previous offenders; and when previous records are disclosed, the office is notified of the offender's past record in order that such information may be passed along to the judge presiding at the trial.

1. A summons cannot be issued in place of an arrest. 1.___

2. Before a summons is issued, an Inspector should make sure 2.___
   of the identity of the offender.

3. Summonses are always returnable to the local District 3.___
   City Civil Court having jurisdiction over the area in
   which the offense was committed.

4. Inspectors should allow at least 24 days to elapse between 4.___
   time of service and time for arraignment.

5. A card is submitted after each tour by an Inspector which, 5.___
   among other things, describes the violator, his address,
   and the violation.

6. The card submitted should also include the place of occur- 6.___
   rence, the court, and the returnable date.

7. The summons cards are checked against a file for previous 7.___
   offenders.

8. When a previous record is disclosed, it is filed in the   8.___
   Magistrates' Court.

9. The officer is notified of a previous record so that the   9.___
   presiding magistrate can be aware of the situation at the
   trial.

10. Summonses are usually issued to men already under arrest.   10.___

11. If a section had 48 miles of street to plow after a   11.___
    snowstorm and 9 plows are used, each plow would cover
    an average of 4 miles.

12. If a crosswalk plow engine is run 5 minutes a day for ten   12.___
    days in a given month, it would run one hour in the course
    of this month.

13. If the department uses 1,500 men in manual street cleaning   13.___
    and half as many more to load and drive trucks, the total
    number used is 2,200 men.

14. If an Inspector issued 186 summonses in the course of 7   14.___
    hours, his hourly average was 25 summonses issued.

15. If an Inspector issued 186 summonses and one hundred were   15.___
    issued to first offenders, then there were 86 summonses
    issued to other than first offenders.

Questions 16-35.

DIRECTIONS: Questions 16 through 35 are to be answered on the basis
             of the material contained in the following passage.

The responsibility of the Bureau of Street Cleaning and Waste
Collection of the Dept. of Sanitation is   to render sanitary service
for approximately 7,500,000 resident taxpayers and 2,500,000 transients who visit the city daily from neighboring states.

Sanitary service includes the collection and removal of refuse,
sweeping, cleaning, washing, and sanding of only those streets under
Department jurisdiction, removal of dead animals, and removal of
snow and ice during the winter season.

For the performance of these functions, the Bureau maintains an
office of the Assistant to Commissioner, a city office, seven borough
offices, sixty-one district offices, and fifty-seven garages, through
which all orders, notices, and directives are transmitted, guiding
the work of the field forces in the performance of their various
assignments.

To maintain close supervision as a medium for obtaining the
utmost in operating efficiency, the Bureau's sixty-one districts
are subdivided into two hundred and forty-eight sections, an average
of approximately four sections per district.

Each district is staffed with a superintendent, foremen, assistant foreman, and other personnel and equipment as is required for the proper performance of work. Districts vary in population from 10,500 to 350,000 persons, a square area ranging from 6/10 mile to 21 miles.

The work is regulated on the basis of established schedules and procedures, variations being introduced at frequent intervals as a means of promoting greater efficiency. Although each district operates as a distinct unit and in accordance with its particular requirements, the scheme of operating is so arranged as to coordinate with the work of adjoining districts. This arrangement follows throughout the various boroughs and provides for the servicing of the entire city.

16. Sanitation districts are subdivided into sections. 16.____

17. There is the same number of borough offices as there are boroughs. 17.____

18. There is a garage attached to each district. 18.____

19. There are approximately four sections to each district. 19.____

20. Each district is headed by a foreman. 20.____

21. The department renders service to approximately 10,000,000 persons daily. 21.____

22. One-third of the city's daily population is composed of transients. 22.____

23. Sanitary service does not include the removal of dead animals. 23.____

24. The Department sweeps and cleans all streets in the city. 24.____

25. Directives to the field forces are transmitted through the district offices. 25.____

26. No district is less than ½ mile square. 26.____

27. No district is more than 21 miles wide. 27.____

28. The largest population of any district is 350,000 people. 28.____

29. The smallest districts have a population of at least 10,500 people. 29.____

30. There is no variation in schedules and procedures. 30.____

31. Snow removal is not handled by the Bureau of Street Cleaning and Waste Collection. 31.____

32. Each district operates as a distinct unit. 32.___

33. If each section has one assistant foreman, there must be at least 248 assistant foremen in the Bureau. 33.___

34. The number of superintendents in this Bureau is at least 61. 34.___

35. Each district coordinates its operations with those of adjoining districts. 35.___

36. In lifting heavy articles, sanitation men should keep their feet wide apart. 36.___

37. Lubricating grease is recommended for treating burns. 37.___

38. Throwing cold water on the face is a good treatment for shock. 38.___

39. A puncture by a nail may lead to lockjaw. 39.___

40. A good first aid remedy for food poisoning is *dilute and wash out*. 40.___

41. If one length of hose is 50 feet, six lengths equal 250 feet. 41.___

42. If the Department has 2 officers to every 18 men, the ratio is 1 to 9. 42.___

43. A street measuring 200' by 36' from curb to curb has an area of 800 sq. yards. 43.___

44. A ton pick-up truck will hold at least 2,000 lbs. 44.___

45. An employee who works from 6 P.M. to 4 A.M. the following morning works a total of 8 hours. 45.___

46. A truck body measuring 5½ feet by 1½ feet by 8 feet has a capacity of 66 cubic feet. 46.___

47. A sanitation truck averaging 18 miles per hour travels approximately 6 miles in 20 minutes. 47.___

48. A sanitation man born July 20, 1928 was 21 years and 22 days old on August 11, 1949. 48.___

49. If 231 cubic inches equal one gallon, then a 2½ gallon fire extinguisher measures about 577.5 cubic inches. 49.___

50. If a scraper costs $1.87, then 100 scrapers will cost $18.70. 50.___

— (#3) —

KEY (CORRECT ANSWERS)

1.	F	11.	F	21.	T	31.	F	41.	F
2.	T	12.	F	22.	F	32.	T	42.	T
3.	T	13.	F	23.	F	33.	T	43.	T
4.	F	14.	F	24.	F	34.	T	44.	T
5.	T	15.	T	25.	T	35.	T	45.	F
6.	T	16.	T	26.	T	36.	F	46.	T
7.	T	17.	F	27.	T	37.	F	47.	T
8.	F	18.	F	28.	T	38.	F	48.	T
9.	T	19.	T	29.	T	39.	T	49.	T
10.	F	20.	F	30.	F	40.	T	50.	F

EXAMINATION SECTION
TEST 1

DIRECTIONS: Each question is a statement. You are to decide whether the statement is TRUE or FALSE.

1. An employee should refuse to carry out an order of his supervisor when he does not agree with its wisdom.

2. A workman should try to learn his foreman's opinions on general affairs so he can agree with them in order to get special advantages over his fellow workmen.

3. Mutual confidence and goodwill among employees of a city department helps the smooth working of the department.

4. When two employees of equal rank disagree about the method of doing certain work, each one should do it in his own way without consulting their supervisor.

5. Physical strength is less important for some city jobs than for others.

6. If you do not entirely understand your supervisor's instructions, you should ask him to repeat and explain them.

7. If a member of the public asks you to do something which the rules of your job don't permit you to do but which is no trouble for you, you might just as well do it to make him happy.

8. If you see a child marking up some public property you should put such a scare into him that he'll be too afraid to do anything like that again.

9. Putting in a good day's work is important, but being on time for work is also important.

10. Courtesy to the public in your job is not important as long as you give good service.

11. It is all right for an employee who feels like quitting early to go home and to explain to his supervisor the next morning.

12. If you do not know the answer to a question that a member of the public asks you, you should admit it.

13. If a member of the public is rude to you while you are at work, you should be just as rude to him.

14. If a member of the public complains to you about how you do your work you should consider whether his complaint is justified

15. In doing your work as a city employee, you should keep in mind that the majority of the public is always ready to criticize you for your work, whether it is well done or not.

16. The public will probably comply more willingly with rules that you must enforce in connection with your job if they understand the need for these rules.

17. It is not desirable for a city employee who works in uniform, in the public eye, to smoke while he is on duty.

18. If, while you are on duty, you hear a call for help you should wait till the call is repeated before you respond.

19. If a member of the public asks you for some general information about the work of your Department, you should advise him to write a letter to your Department even though you have this information.

20. Many times a person's opinion about a City Department is influenc by the impression he gets of the employees of that Department.

21. If you and another employee are assigned to the same work and he can't put out as much work as you, you should try not to do more than he does so as not to make him look bad.

22. If you must turn in a written report to your supervisor about something that happened on the job it is a good idea to turn it in as soon as possible after the incident so that the facts will be fresh in your mind.

23. A new employee who has a problem or grievance about his work or working conditions should not hesitate to take it up with his supervisor.

24. If a city employee understands the aims and purposes of his department, it is likely to help him do his job better.

25. Supervisors expect new employees to make many mistakes in their first year or two of work.

Questions 26-32.

DIRECTIONS: Questions 26 through 32 are to be answered only on the basis of the information contained in the following paragraph.

RESPONSIBILITY OF PARENTS

In a recent survey, ninety percent of the people interviewed felt that parents should be held responsible for the delinquency of their children. Forty-eight out of fifty states have laws holding parents criminally responsible for contributing to the delinquency of their children. It is generally accepted that parents are a major influenc in the early moral development of their children. Yet, in spite of all this evidence, practical experience seems to prove that "punish the parents" laws are wrong. Legally, there is some question about the constitutionality of such laws. How far can one person be held responsible for the actions of another? Further, although there are many such laws, the fact remains that they are rarely used and where they are used, they fail in most cases to accomplish the end for which they were intended.

26. Nine out of ten of those interviewed held that parents should be responsible for the delinquency of their children.

27. Forty-eight percent of the states have laws holding parents responsible for contributing to the delinquency of their children.

28. Most people feel that parents have little influence on the early moral development of their children.

29. Experience seems to indicate that laws holding parents responsible for children's delinquency are wrong.

30. There is no doubt that laws holding parents responsible for delinquency of their children are within the constitution.

31. Laws holding parents responsible for delinquent children are not often enforced.

32. "Punish the parent" laws usually achieve their purpose.

Questions 33-38.

DIRECTIONS: Questions 33 through 38 are to be answered only on the basis of the information contained in the following paragraph.

CONTROL OF RABIES

The history of rabies in many countries proves the need for strong preventive measures. England is a good example. Rabies ran rampant in the British Isles during the American Revolution. In the 19th century, the country began to enforce strict measures: licensing all dogs, muzzling all dogs and quarantining all incoming animals for 6 months' observation. An additional measure was the capturing and killing of all unlicensed "strays".

As a result, rabies was completely eradicated, and similar measures have achieved the same results in Ireland, Denmark, Norway, Sweden, Australia and Hawaii.

33. Rabies was prevalent in England about the year 1776.

34. By enforcement of strict measures in the 1800's rabies was eliminated in England.

35. The only measures enforced in England for the control of rabies were the licensing and muzzling of all dogs.

36. Unlicensed dogs without owners were put to death when found.

37. A total of six countries, including England, obtained good results in combating rabies.

38. In three Scandinavian countries rabies has been eliminated.

Questions 39-50.

DIRECTIONS: Questions 39 through 50 are to be answered only on the
basis of the information contained in the following
paragraph.

RESCUE BREATHING

Mouth-to-mouth, or rescue breathing , is the easiest, most
efficient and quickest method of getting oxygen into a suffocating
victim of drowning, heart attack, electrical shock, poisoning or
other cause of interruption of breathing. It is superior to other
types of artificial respiration because the victim does not have
to be moved and the rescuer can continue for hours without exhaustion. No special equipment is needed.

Begin rescue breathing immediately. The victim's head should be
lower than his body. Tilt his head back as far as possible so his
jaw justs out. Keep the air passage to his lungs straight at all
times. Open your mouth as wide as possible and seal your lips over
the adult victim's mouth or his nose and the child victim's mouth
and nose. Blow in air until his chest rises. Remove your mouth and
listen to him breathe out. Then blow again and fill his lungs.

For the first minute blow thirty times into a child, then twenty
times a minute. With an adult, blow twenty times for the first minute
then ten to twelve times a minute. Do not stop breathing for the
victim, however long it takes, until he begins breathing for himself -- or is dead.

39. The fastest way to get oxygen into the lungs of a suffocating
person is by mouth-to-mouth breathing.

40. The rescue breathing method of artificial respiration should
be used only in cases of drowning.

41. Rescue breathing is not the only kind of artificial respiration.

42. The person who applies mouth-to-mouth breathing will not tire
easily.

43. Special equipment used in rescue breathing should be kept
handy at all times.

44. Rescue breathing should be commenced at the earliest possible
moment.

45. The suffocating victim should be placed so that his body is
not higher than his head.

46. In rescue breathing , the head of the victim should be bent
forward so oxygen will be more easily forced into his lungs.

47. In mouth-to-mouth breathing air may be blown into the victim's
nose.

48. When rescue breathing is applied to children air should be blown into the lungs thirty times during the first minute.

49. It is never necessary to continue rescue breathing for longer than about five minutes.

50. Mouth-to-mouth breathing is always successful in reviving the victim.

———

KEY (CORRECT ANSWERS)

1.	F	11.	F	21.	F	31.	T	41.	T
2.	F	12.	T	22.	T	32.	F	42.	T
3.	T	13.	F	23.	T	33.	T	43.	F
4.	F	14.	T	24.	T	34.	T	44.	T
5.	T	15.	F	25.	F	35.	F	45.	F
6.	T	16.	T	26.	T	36.	T	46.	F
7.	F	17.	T	27.	F	37.	F	47.	T
8.	F	18.	F	28.	F	38.	T	48.	T
9.	T	19.	F	29.	T	39.	T	49.	F
10.	F	20.	T	30.	F	40.	F	50.	F

———

TEST 2

DIRECTIONS: Each question is a statement. You are to decide whether the statement is TRUE or FALSE.

1. "His ideas about the best method of doing the work were flexible." In this sentence, the word 'flexible' means NEARLY the same as 'unchangeable'.

2. "Many difficulties were encountered." In this sentence, the word 'encountered' means NEARLY the same as 'met'.

3. "The different parts of the refuse must be segregated." In this sentence, the word 'segregated' means NEARLY the same as 'combined'.

4. "The child was obviously hurt." In this sentence, the word 'obviously' means NEARLY the same as 'accidentally'.

5. "Some kind of criteria for judging service necessity must be established." In this sentence, the word 'criteria' means NEARLY the same as 'standards'.

6. "A small segment of the membership favored the amendment." In this sentence, the word 'segment' means NEARLY the same as 'part'.

7. "The effectiveness of any organization depends upon the quality and integrity of its rank and file." In this sentence, the word 'integrity' means NEARLY the same as 'quantity'.

8. "He adhered to his opinion." In this sentence, the word 'adhered' means NEARLY the same as 'stuck to'.

9. "The suspects were interrogated at the police station." In this sentence, 'interrogated' means NEARLY the same as 'identified'.

10. "Flanking the fireplace are shelves holding books." In this sentence, the word 'flanking' means NEARLY the same as 'above'.

11. "He refused to comment on the current Berlin crisis." In this sentence, the word 'current' means NEARLY the same as 'shocking'.

12. "Nothing has been done to remedy the situation." In this sentence, the word 'remedy' means NEARLY the same as 'correct'.

13. "The reports had been ignored." In this sentence, the word 'ignored' means NEARLY the same as 'prepared'.

14. "A firm was hired to construct the building." In this sentence, the word 'construct' means NEARLY the same as 'build'.

15. "The Commissioner spoke about the operations of his department." In this sentence, the word 'operations' means NEARLY the same as 'problems'.

16. "The metal was corroded." In this sentence, the word 'corroded' means NEARLY the same as 'polished'.

17. "The price of this merchandise fluctuates from day to day." In this sentence, the word 'fluctuates' means the OPPOSITE of 'remains steady'.

18. "The patient was in acute pain." In this sentence, the word 'acute' means the OPPOSITE of 'slight'.

19. "The essential data appear in the report." In this sentence, the word 'data' means the OPPOSITE of 'facts'.

20. "The open lounge is spacious." In this sentence, the word 'spacious means the OPPOSITE of 'well-lighted'.

21. A good first aid measure for a person who has fainted is to place his head lower than the rest of the body.

22. Many accidents are caused by carelessness of employees while at work.

23. If, at work, you are unable to lift a very heavy object, you should rest a couple of minutes and try again.

24. A victim of a bad fall who has suffered some broken bones should be moved to a comfortable spot immediately.

25. The safest and quickest way to remove a burnt-out light bulb from a ceiling fixture is to stand on a chair on top of a desk or table.

26. When using soaps, powders, or wax, it is a good idea to follow the rule, if a little of the material is good, more of the material is still better.

27. More accidents occur as the result of unsafe acts of cleaners than as a result of unsafe conditions and surroundings.

28. Oily rags should be kept in self-closing containers.

29. A cleaner should be instructed to keep the drain spigot open when filling a mop truck with water.

30. A cleaner should not climb higher than the third step from the top of a ladder when cleaning a wall.

31. A knife may be properly used as a can opener if the tip of the blade is blunt or not pointed.

32. Ink stains on wood desks which do not respond to soap and water may be removed with kerosene.

33. A good way to remove paint from window glass is to rub it with fine sandpaper.

34. There is a greater danger of shock when electric fixtures and wires are touched with dry hands than with wet hands.

35. Modern cleaning methods considers the use of deodorants in washrooms necessary and desirable in most instances.

36. Generally, the last part of the routine cleaning and maintaining of a washroom is mopping, rinsing, and drying the floor.

37. Urinal strainers are removed daily and drainage pipes cleaned with a spoke brush in the routine cleaning of washrooms.

38. If three men working at the same rate of speed finish a job in 4 1/2 hours, then two of them could do the job in 6 3/4 hours

39. If a typist shares four boxes of envelopes with four other typists, each will have one box of envelopes.

40. An article bought for $100 must be sold for $125 in order to make a profit of 20% of the selling price.

41. 1/2 of 1/8 is 1/4.

42. Ten square feet of carpet will cover the floor of a room 10 feet by 10 feet.

Questions 43-50.

DIRECTIONS: Questions 43-50 are to be answered ONLY on the basis of the information contained in the following table.

SUMMONS RECORD

| District | No. of Summonses Issued | | No. Dismissed | |
	1981	1982	1981	1982
Oakdale	3,250	3,147	650	631
Marlboro	2,410	2,320	670	718
Eastchester	3,502	3,710	800	825
Kensington	10,423	10,218	2,317	2,343
Glenridge	5,100	5,250	1,200	1,213
Seaside	4,864	4,739	1,469	1,375
Darwin	3,479	3,661	815	826
Ulster	4,100	3,789	1,025	1,000
Totals	37,128	?	8,946	?

43. In most of the districts, the number of summonses dismissed was greater in 1982 than in 1981.

44. In most of the districts, the number of summonses issued was smaller in 1981 than in 1982.

45. The district which had the smallest number of summonses issued in 1981, also had the smallest number of summonses dismissed in 1981.

46. The two districts which issued the largest number of summonses in 1982 also dismissed the largest number of summonses in 1982.

47. The district that was second in the number of summonses issued both years was also second in the number of summonses dismissed both years.

48. The total number of summonses dismissed in 1982 is 15 less than the total number dismissed in 1981.

49. In 1982 there was a greater difference between the two districts with the smallest and largest number of summonses dismissed than in 1981.

50. The total number of summonses issued in 1981 is 294 greater than the total number of summonses issued in 1982.

KEY (CORRECT ANSWERS)

1.	F	11.	F	21.	T	31.	F	41.	F
2.	T	12.	T	22.	T	32.	F	42.	F
3.	F	13.	F	23.	F	33.	F	43.	T
4.	F	14.	T	24.	F	34.	F	44.	F
5.	T	15.	F	25.	F	35.	F	45.	F
6.	T	16.	F	26.	F	36.	T	46.	F
7.	F	17.	T	27.	T	37.	F	47.	F
8.	T	18.	T	28.	T	38.	T	48.	T
9.	F	19.	F	29.	F	39.	F	49.	T
10.	F	20.	F	30.	T	40.	T	50.	T

EXAMINATION SECTION
TEST 1

DIRECTIONS: Each question or incomplete statement is followed by
several suggested answers or completions. Select the
one that *BEST* answers the question or completes the
statement. *PRINT THE LETTER OF THE CORRECT ANSWER IN
THE SPACE AT THE RIGHT.*

Questions 1 - 4.

DIRECTIONS: Answer Questions 1 through 4 on the basis of the information provided in the paragraph below.

Rodent control must be planned carefully in order to insure its
success. This means that more knowledge is needed about the habits
and favorite breeding places of Domestic Rats, than any other kind.
A favorite breeding place for Domestic Rats is known to be in old
or badly constructed buildings. Rats find these buildings very
comfortable for making nests. However, the only way to gain this
kind of detailed knowledge about rats is through careful study.

1. According to the above paragraph, rats find comfortable   1.___
   nesting places
     A. in old buildings   B. in pipes
     C. on roofs   D. in sewers

2. The paragraph states that the *BEST* way to learn all about 2.___
   the favorite nesting places of rats is by
     A. asking people   B. careful study
     C. using traps   D. watching ratholes

3. According to the paragraph, in order to insure the success   3.___
   of rodent control, it is necessary to
     A. design better bait   B. give out more information
     C. plan carefully   D. use pesticides

4. The paragraph states that the *MOST* important rats to   4.___
   study are
     A. African Rats   B. Asian Rats
     C. Domestic Rats   D. European Rats

Questions 5 - 8.

DIRECTIONS: Answer Questions 5 through 8 on the basis of the
following paragraph.

A few people who live in old tenements have the bad habit of
throwing garbage out of their windows, especially if there is an
empty lot near their building. Sometimes the garbage is food, sometimes the garbage is half-empty soda cans. Sometimes the garbage
is a little bit of both mixed together. These people just don't
care about keeping the lot clean.

5. The paragraph states that throwing garbage out of windows   5.___
   is a
     A. bad habit   B. dangerous thing to do
     C. good thing to do   D. good way to feed rats

6. According to the paragraph, an empty lot next to an old   6.___
   tenement, is sometimes used as a place to
   A. hold local gang meetings   B. play ball
   C. throw garbage   D. walk dogs

7. According to the paragraph, which of the following throw   7.___
   garbage out of their windows?
   A. Nobody   B. Everybody   C. Most people D. Some people

8. According to the paragraph, the kinds of garbage thrown   8.___
   out of windows are
   A. candy and cigarette butts
   B. food and half-empty soda cans
   C. fruit and vegetables
   D. rice and bread

Questions 9 - 12.

DIRECTIONS: Answer Questions 9 through 12 on the basis of the
               following paragraph.

   The game that is recognized all over the world as an all-
American game is the game of baseball. As a matter of fact, baseball heroes like Joe DiMaggio, Willie Mays and Babe Ruth were as
famous in their day as movie stars Robert Redford, Paul Newman and
Clint Eastwood are now. All these men have had the experience of
being mobbed by fans whenever they put in an appearance anywhere
in the world. Such unusual popularity makes it possible for stars
like these to earn at least as much money off the job as on the
job. It didn't take manufacturers and advertising men long to
discover that their sales of shaving lotion, for instance, increased when they got famous stars to advertise their product for
them on radio and television.

9. According to the paragraph, baseball is known everywhere   9.___
   as a(n)
   A. all-American game   B. fast game
   C. unusual game   D. tough game

10. According to the paragraph, being so well known means   10.___
    that it is possible for people like Willie Mays and
    Babe Ruth to
    A. ask for anything and get it
    B. make as much money off the job as on it
    C. travel anywhere free of charge
    D. watch any game free of charge

11. According to the paragraph, which of the following are   11.___
    known all over the world?
    A. Baseball heroes   B. Advertising men
    C. Manufacturers   D. Basketball heroes

12. According to the paragraph, it is possible to sell much   12.___
    more shaving lotion on television and radio if
    A. the commercials are in color instead of black and
       white
    B. you can get a prize with each bottle of shaving lotion
    C. the shaving lotion makes you smell nicer than usual
    D. the shaving lotion is advertised by famous stars

Questions 13 - 16.

DIRECTIONS: Answer Questions 13 through 16 on the basis of the
               following paragraph.

People are very suspicious of all strangers who knock at their
door. For this reason every pest control aide, whether man or woman,
must carry an identification card at all times on the job. These
cards are issued by the agency the aide works for. The aide's picture is on the card. The aide's name is typed in and the aide's sig-
nature is written on the line below. The name, address and telephone
number of the agency issuing the card is also printed on it. Once
the aide shows this ID card to prove his or her identity, the tenant's
time should not be taken up with small talk. The tenant should be
told briefly what pest control means. The aide should be polite and
ready to answer any questions the tenant may have on the subject.
Then, the aide should thank the tenant for listening and say goodbye.

13. According to the above paragraph, when she visits ten-   13.___
     ants, the one item a pest control aide must *always* carry
     with her is a(n)
        A. badge   B. driver's license
        C. identification card   D. watch

14. According to the paragraph, a pest control aide is sup-   14.___
     posed to talk to each tenant he visits
        A. at length about the agency
        B. briefly about pest control
        C. at length about family matters
        D. briefly about social security

15. According to the paragraph, the item that does *NOT* appear   15.___
     on an ID card is the
        A. address of the agency   B. name of the agency
        C. signature of the aide
        D. social security number of the aide

16. According to the paragraph, a pest control aide carries   16.___
     an identification card because he must
        A. prove to tenants who he is
        B. provide the tenant with the agency's address
        C. provide the tenant with the agency's telephone number
        D. save the tenant's time

Questions 17 - 20.

DIRECTIONS: Questions 17 through 20 are to be answered on the basis
               of the following paragraph.

Very early on a summer's morning, the nicest thing to look at is
a beach, before the swimmers arrive. Usually all the litter has been
picked up from the sand by the Park Department clean-up crew. Everything is quiet. All you can hear are the waves breaking, and the sea
gulls calling to each other. The beach opens to the public at 10 a.m.
Long before that time, however, long lines of eager men, women and
children have driven up to the entrance. They form long lines that
wind around the beach waiting for the signal to move.

17. According to the paragraph, before 10 a.m., long lines   17.___
    are formed that are made up of
    A. cars   B. clean-up crews
    C. men, women and children D. Park Department trucks

18. The season referred to in the above paragraph is   18.___
    A. fall   B. summer   C. winter   D. spring

19. The place the paragraph is describing is a   19.___
    A. beach   B. park
    C. golf course   D. tennis court

20. According to the paragraph, one of the things you notice, 20.___
    early in the morning, is that
    A. radios are playing   B. swimmers are there
    C. the sand is dirty   D. the litter is gone

Questions 21 - 30.

DIRECTIONS: In Questions 21 through 30, select the answer which
             means *most nearly* the *SAME* as the capitalized word
             in the sentence.

21. He received a large REWARD. In this sentence the word   21.___
    REWARD means
    A. capture   B. recompense C. key   D. praise

22. The aide was asked to TRANSMIT a message. In this sen- 22.___
    tence the word TRANSMIT means
    A. change   B. send   C. take   D. type

23. The pest control aide REQUESTED the tenant to call the   23.___
    Health Department. In this sentence, the word REQUESTED
    means the pest control aide
    A. asked   B. helped   C. informed   D. warned

24. The driver had to RETURN the Health Department's truck.   24.___
    In this sentence, the word RETURN means
    A. borrow   B. fix   C. give back D. load up

25. The aide discussed the PURPOSE of the visit. In this   25.___
    sentence, the word PURPOSE means
    A. date   B. hour   C. need   D. reason

26. The tenant SUSPECTED the aide who knocked at her door.   26.___
    In this sentence, the word SUSPECTED means
    A. answered   B. called   C. distrusted D. welcomed

27. The aide was POSITIVE that the child hit her. In this   27.___
    sentence, the word POSITIVE means
    A. annoyed   B. certain   C. sorry   D. surprised

28. The tenant DECLINED to call the Health Department. In   28.___
    this sentence DECLINED means
    A. agreed   B. decided   C. refused   D. wanted

29. The aide ARRIVED on time. In this sentence, the word ARRIVED means   29.___

    A. awoke   B. came   C left   D. delayed

30. The salesman had to DELIVER books to each person he   30.___
    visited. In this sentence, the word DELIVER means

    A. give   B. lend   C. mail   D. sell

KEY (CORRECT ANSWERS)

1.	A	11.	A	21.	B
2.	B	12.	D	22.	B
3.	C	13.	C	23.	A
4.	C	14.	B	24.	C
5.	A	15.	D	25.	D
6.	C	16.	A	26.	C
7.	D	17.	C	27.	B
8.	B	18.	B	28.	C
9.	A	19.	A	29.	B
10.	B	20.	D	30.	A

TEST 2

DIRECTIONS: Each question or incomplete statement is followed by several suggested answers or completions. Select the one that *BEST* answers the question or completes the statement. *PRINT THE LETTER OF THE CORRECT ANSWER IN THE SPACE AT THE RIGHT.*

Questions 1 - 10.

DIRECTIONS: In Questions 1 through 10 pick the word that means *most nearly* the *OPPOSITE* of the capitalized word in the sentence.

1. It is possible to CONSTRUCT a rat-proof home. The opposite of CONSTRUCT is
   A. build   B. erect   C. plant   D. wreck   1.___

2. The pest control aide had to REPAIR the flat tire. The opposite of the word REPAIR is
   A. destroy   B. fix   C. mend   D. patch   2.___

3. The pest control aide tried to SHOUT the answer. The opposite of the word SHOUT is
   A. scream   B. shriek   C. whisper   D. yell   3.___

4. Daily VISITS are the best. The opposite of the word VISITS is
   A. absences   B. exercises   C. lessons   D. trials   4.___

5. It is important to ARRIVE early in the morning. The opposite of the word ARRIVE is
   A. climb   B. descend   C. enter   D. leave   5.___

6. Jorge is a group LEADER. The opposite of the word LEADER is
   A. boss   B. chief   C. follower   D. overseer   6.___

7. The EXTERIOR of the house needs painting. The opposite of the word EXTERIOR is
   A. inside   B. outdoors   C. outside   D. surface   7.___

8. He CONCEDED the victory. The opposite of the word CONCEDED is
   A. admitted   B. denied   C. granted   D. reported   8.___

9. He watched the team BEGIN. The opposite of the word BEGIN is
   A. end   B. fail   C. gather   D. win   9.___

10. Your handwriting is ILLEGIBLE. The opposite of the word ILLEGIBLE is
    A. clear   B. confused   C. jumbled   D. unclear   10.___

Questions 11 - 15.

DIRECTIONS: Answer Question 11 through 15 by following the instructions given in each question. Note that 5 possible answers have been given for these questions *ONLY*. Therefore, for these questions your choice may be A, B, C, D or E.

11. Add: 12 1/2   11.___
           2 1/4
           3 1/4

     The correct answer is:
     A. 17   B. 17 1/4 C. 17 1/2 D. 17 3/4 E. 18

12. Subtract: 150   12.___
              - 80

     The correct answer is:
     A. 70   B. 80   C. 130   D. 150   E. 230

13. After cleaning up some lots in the East Bronx, five   13.___
     clean-up crews loaded the following amounts of garbage
     on trucks:
               Crew No. 1 loaded 2 1/4 tons
               Crew No. 2 loaded 3   tons
               Crew No. 3 loaded 1 1/4 tons
               Crew No. 4 loaded 2 1/4 tons
               Crew No. 5 loaded   1/2 ton

     The *TOTAL* number of tons of garbage loaded was
     A. 8   B. 8 1/4   C. 8 3/4   D. 9   E. 9 1/4

14. Subtract: 17 3/4   14.___
              - 7 1/4

     The correct answer is:
     A. 7 1/2   B. 10 1/2 C. 14 1/4 D. 17 3/4 E. 25

15. Yesterday Tom and Bill each received 10 leaflets about   15.___
     rat control. Each supermarket in the neighborhood was
     supposed to receive one of these leaflets. When the day
     was over, Tom had 8 leaflets left. Bill had no leaflets
     left. How many supermarkets got leaflets yesterday?
     A. 8   B. 10   C. 12   D. 18   E. 20

Questions 16 - 20.

DIRECTIONS: Answer Questions 16 through 20 ONLY on the basis of the
             information in the statement and chart on page 3, DAILY
             WORK REPORT FORM (Chart A).

     Assume that you are a member of Pest Control Truck Crew Number 1.
Julio Rivera is your Crew Chief. The crew is supposed to report to
work at nine o'clock in the morning. Since you are the first to show
up, at ten minutes before nine, on 5/24/74 Rivera asks you to help him
out by filling in the Daily Work Report Form for him. Driver Hal Williams shows up at nine and Driver Rick Smith shows up ten minutes
after Williams.

16. According to the statement above, the entry that belongs   16.___
     in Block #9 is
          A. Julio Rivera   B. June Stevens
          C. Jim Watson   D. Hal Williams

DAILY WORK REPORT FORM (Chart A)

Block #1	Block #2	
Crew No:	Date	

Block #3 TRUCKS IN USE	Block #4 DRIVER'S NAME	Block #5	TIME OF ARRIVAL
		A.M.	P.M.
Truck # _____	_____		
# _____	_____		
# _____	_____		
# _____	_____		
# _____	_____		
# _____	_____		
# _____	_____		
# _____	_____		
# _____	_____		

Block #6 TRUCKS OUT OF ORDER	Block #7 ADDRESS OF CLEAN-UP SITE	Block #8
Truck # _____	No. _____	Borough
# _____	Street _____	Block #9
# _____	_____	Signature of Crew Chief

16. According to the statement above, the entry that belongs in 16. ____
     Block #9 is
         A. Julio Rivera B. June Stevens C. Jim Watson D. Hal Williams
17. According to the above statement the entry that should be 17. ____
     made in Block #2 is
         A. 9:00 a.m. B. 9:10 p.m.   C. 5/24/74   D. 7/24/74

18. The names of Hal Williams and Rick Smith should appear in 18. ____
         A. Block #4   B. Block #6   C. Block #7   D. Block #9

19. Rick Smith's time of arrival should be entered in Block· 19.___
    #5 as
       A. 8:50 a.m.   B. 8:55 a.m.   C. 9:00 a.m.   D. 9:10 a.m.

20. According to the statement, the entry that should be made 20.___
    in Block #1 is
       A. zero   B. one   C. 5/24/74   D. 6/24/74

Questions 21 - 23.

DIRECTIONS: Answer Questions 21 through 23 on the basis of the
              statement shown below. Use DAILY WORK REPORT FORM
              (Chart A) on page 3, as a guide.

    Pete Marberg showed up at a quarter after nine, in the morning,
but his truck, No. 22632441, was in the garage for repairs. Steve
Marino showed up a half hour after Pete. He was assigned truck
No. 6342003, which was in working order.

21. According to the above statement, truck No. 22632441   21.___
    should be entered in
       A. Block #3   B. Block #4   C. Block #6   D. Block #8

22. According to the above statement, Steve Marino showed up 22.___
    at
       A. 9:00 a.m.   B. 9:15 a.m.   C. 9:30 p.m.   D. 9:45 a.m.

23. According to the above statement, Steve Marino's truck   23.___
    number belongs in Block #3. The number entered there
    should be
       A. #22632441 B. #6342003   C. #6432003   D. #26232441

Questions 24 - 30.

DIRECTIONS: Answer Questions 24 through 30 ONLY on the basis of the
              information in the statements above each question and
              the chart on page 5, DAILY GARBAGE COLLECTION REPORT
              (Chart B).

24. Truck #2437752 started unloading garbage at ten o'clock   24.___
    Monday morning and finished unloading its garbage that
    afternoon. The clock looked like this when the job was
    done.

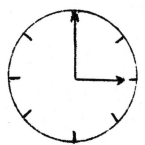

The time entries that should be recorded in Block #5
are
       A. 10 a.m. and 12:15 p.m.   B. 10 p.m. and 12:30 a.m.
       C. 10 p.m. and 12:00 a.m.   D. 10 a.m. and 3:00 p.m.

DAILY GARBAGE COLLECTION REPORT (Chart B)

Block #1 No. of trucks Used For Collection	Block #2 Address of Garbage Pick-Up	Block #3 Amount of Garbage Collected	Block #4 Amount of Garbage Unloaded	Block #5 Hours During Which Garbage Was Unloaded
#456	45 South-west	1/2 ton	1/2 ton	From 7 a.m. To 8 a.m.

	Block #6 Total Amount of Garbage Collected By All Trucks	Block #7 Total Amount of Garbage Unloaded By All Trucks	Block #8 Total Amount of Time Spent Unloading Of All Trucks
TOTALS			

25. Truck #8967432 had to pick up a load of garbage from 911 South Avenue. It took the crew until 11:00 a.m. to load the garbage.

    According to this statement, the item 911 South Avenue should be entered in
      A. Block #1   B. Block #2   C. Block #3   D. Block #4

25.___

26. On Tuesday, truck #124356 unloaded 1/2 ton of garbage, truck #2437752 unloaded 1/4 ton of garbage and truck #435126 unloaded 1 ton of garbage. The *TOTAL AMOUNT* of garbage unloaded by the three trucks on Tuesday should be entered in
      A. Block #3   B. Block #4   C. Block #5   D. Block #8

26.___

27. On Wednesday, it took truck #4050607 from 2 p.m. to 6 p.m. to unload 1 ton of garbage. It took truck #7040650 from 1 p.m. to 2 p.m. to unload 1/4 ton of garbage. These were the only trucks working that day. The *TOTAL AMOUNT* of time it took for both trucks to unload garbage was
      A. 5 hours   B. 6 hours   C. 7 hours   D. 8 hours

27.___

28. The amount of garbage collected by one truck should be   28.___
    entered in the DAILY GARBAGE COLLECTION REPORT form in
        A. Block #3   B. Block #6   C. Block #7   D. Block #8

29. Truck #557799010 reported to 1020 Hudson Rivery Alley to   29.___
    pick up garbage from an empty lot. This information
    should be entered in the DAILY GARBAGE COLLECTION REPORT
    form in
        A. Block #1 and Block #4   B. Block #2 and Block #5
        C. Block #1 and Block #2   D. Block #2 and Block #3

30. It took the Pest Control Truck Crew from 8 in the morning   30.___
    to 12 noon to unload the garbage it collected the night
    before. This information should be entered in the DAILY
    GARBAGE COLLECTION REPORT form under
        A. Block #4   B. Block #5   C. Block #6   D. Block #7

KEY (CORRECT ANSWERS)

1.	D		11.	E		21.	C
2.	A		12.	A		22.	D
3.	C		13.	E		23.	B
4.	A		14.	B		24.	D
5.	D		15.	C		25.	B
6.	C		16.	A		26.	B
7.	A		17.	C		27.	A
8.	B		18.	A		28.	A
9.	A		19.	D		29.	C
10.	A		20.	B		30.	B

EXAMINATION SECTION
TEST 1

DIRECTIONS: Each question or incomplete statement is followed by several suggested answers or completions. Select the one that BEST answers the question or completes the statement. *PRINT THE LETTER OF THE CORRECT ANSWER IN THE SPACE AT THE RIGHT*.

1. An employee who is not sure how to do a job that the supervisor has just assigned should   1.____
   A. ask another employee how to do the job
   B. ask the supervisor how to do the job
   C. do some other work until the supervisor gives further instructions
   D. do the best he can

2. An employee who is asked by the supervisor to work one hour overtime cannot stay because of previous arrangements made with the family. The employee should   2.____
   A. ask another employee who does not have a family to take over
   B. explain the situation to the supervisor and ask to be excused
   C. go home, but leave a note for the supervisor explaining the reason for not being able to stay
   D. refuse, giving the excuse that time-and-a-half is not being paid for overtime

3. A department's MAIN purpose in setting up employee rules and regulations is to   3.____
   A. explain the department's work to the public
   B. give an official history of the department
   C. help in the efficient running of the department
   D. limit the number of employees who break the rules

4. The MAIN reason an employee should be polite is that   4.____
   A. he may get into trouble if he is not polite
   B. he never knows when he may be talking to an official
   C. politeness is a duty which any employee owes the public
   D. politeness will make him appear to be alert and efficient

5. Public employees would *most probably* be expected by their supervisor to do   5.____
   A. a fair day's work according to their ability
   B. more work than the employees of other supervisors
   C. more work than the supervisor really knows they can do
   D. the same amount of work that a little better than average employee can do

6. Your supervisor gives you a special job to do without saying when it must be finished and then leaves for another job location. A little before quitting time you realize that you will not be able to finish the job that day. You should   6.____
    A. ask a few of the other employees to help you finish the job
    B. go home at quitting time and finish the job the next day
    C. stay on the job till you get in touch with your supervisor by phone and get further instructions
    D. work overtime till you finish the job

7. "While on duty an employee is not permitted to smoke in public." Of the following, the *most likely* reason for such a rule is that   7.____
    A. government employees must be willing to surrender some of their personal liberties
    B. lighted cigarettes create a fire hazard
    C. nicotine in tobacco will lessen a city employee's ability to perform assigned duties properly
    D. smoking on duty may make an unfavorable impression on the public

8. While you are on duty someone asks you how to get somewhere. Supposing that you know how to get there, you should   8.____
    A. give him the necessary directions
    B. make believe you did not hear him
    C. tell him it is not your duty to give information
    D. tell him you are too busy to give the information

9. The BEST way to make sure that a piece of important mail will be received is to send it by   9.____
    A. first class mail   B. fourth class mail
    C. registered mail   D. special delivery

10. Letters, if they don't weigh more than an ounce, need a   10.____
    A. 17¢ stamp   B. 20¢ stamp
    C. 22¢ stamp   D. 25¢ stamp

QUESTIONS 11-15.
Answer questions 11 to 15 *ONLY* on the basis of the information given in the following paragraph.

 If an employee thinks he can save money, time, or material for the city or has an idea about how to do something better than it is being done, he should not keep it to himself. He should send his ideas to the Employee's Suggestion Program, using the special form which is kept on hand in all departments. An employee may send in as many ideas as he wishes. To make sure that each idea is judged fairly, the name of the suggestor is not made known until an award is made. The awards are certificates of merit or cash prizes ranging from $10 to $500.

11. According to the above paragraph, an employee who knows   11.____
    how to do a job in a better way should
       A. be sure it saves enough time to be worthwhile
       B. get paid the money he saves for the city
       C. keep it to himself to avoid being accused of causing
          a speed-up
       D. send his ideas to the Employee's Suggestion Program

12. In order to send his idea to the Employee's Suggestion   12.____
    Program, an employee should
       A. ask the Department of Personnel for a special form
       B. get the special form in his own department
       C. mail the idea, using Special Delivery
       D. send it on plain, white, letter-sized paper

13. An employee may send to the Employee's Suggestion Program 13.____
       A. as many ideas as he can think of
       B. no more than one idea each week
       C. no more than ten ideas in a month
       D. only one idea on each part of the job

14. The reason the name of an employee who makes a suggestion 14.____
    is not made known at first is to
       A. give the employee a larger award
       B. help the judges give more awards
       C. insure fairness in judging
       D. make sure no employee gets two awards

15. An employee whose suggestion receives an award may be   15.____
    given a
       A. bonus once a year
       B. cash price of up to $500
       C. certificate for $10
       D. salary increase of $500

QUESTIONS 16-18.
Answer questions 16 to 18 *ONLY* on the basis of the information
given in the following paragraph.

According to the rules of the Department of Personnel, the work
of every permanent City employee is reviewed and rated by his
supervisor at least once a year. The civil service rating system
gives the employee and his supervisor a chance to talk about the
progress made during the past year as well as about those parts of
the job in which the employee needs to do better. In order to
receive a pay increase each year, the employee must have a satisfactory service rating. Service ratings also count toward an
employee's final mark on a promotion examination.

16. According to the above paragraph, a permanent City   16.____
    employee is rated *at least* once
       A. before his work is reviewed
       B. every six months
       C. yearly by his supervisor
       D. yearly by the Department of Personnel

17. According to the above paragraph, under the rating system   17.____
    the supervisor and the employee can discuss how
      A. much more work needs to be done next year
      B. the employee did his work last year
      C. the work can be made easier next year
      D. the work of the Department can be increased

18. According to the above paragraph, a permanent City   18.____
    employee will NOT receive a yearly pay increase
      A. if he received a pay increase for the year before
      B. if he used his service rating for his mark on a
         promotion examination
      C. if his service rating is unsatisfactory
      D. unless he got some kind of a service rating

19. "Employees on duty represent their Department to the   19.____
    citizens and are expected to be neat and orderly in their
    dress at all times." According to this statement, neat
    and orderly dress of employees while on duty is important
    because
      A. citizens don't care about the appearance of city
         employees who are off duty
      B. employees who are neat and orderly in their dress
         make better citizens
      C. if an employee dresses neatly while at work, he will
         dress neatly when away from work
      D. people might judge a department by the appearance of
         its employees

20. "In the city there are 266 shoe factories which employ   20.____
    10,000 workers while in all the other cities of the
    state there are 62 shoe factories which employ 27,000
    workers." According to this statement, the shoe factories
    in the city
      A. are larger than the shoe factories in any other
         city in the state
      B. employ more workers than all the other shoe factories
         in the state
      C. make cheaper shoes than the shoe factories in other
         cities of the state
      D. are greater in number than the shoe factories in all
         the other cities of the state

21. "All mail matter up to and including eight ounces in   21.____
    weight which is not classified as first or second class
    mail is third class mail. If a package weighs more than
    eight ounces, it is put into the fourth class and sent as
    parcel-post mail." According to this statement, mail
    weighing eight ounces or less may be
      A. classified as parcel-post mail
      B. first, second, or third class mail
      C. second class mail but not third class
      D. third or fourth class mail

QUESTIONS 22-24.
Answer questions 22 to 24 *ONLY* on the basis of the information
given in the following paragraph.

Keeping the City of New York operating day and night requires the
services of more than 200,000 civil service workers - roughly the
number of people who live in Syracuse. This huge army of specialists work at more than 2,000 different jobs. The City's civil
service workers are able to do everything that needs doing to keep
the City running. Their only purpose is the well-being, comfort
and safety of the citizens of New York.

22. Of the following titles, the one that *most nearly* gives   22._____
    the meaning of the above paragraph is:
    A. "Civil Service in Syracuse"
    B. "Everyone Works"
    C. "Job Variety"
    D. "Serving New York City"

23. According to the above paragraph, in order to keep New   23._____
    York City operating 24 hours a day
    A. half of the civil service workers work days and
       half work nights
    B. more than 200,000 civil service workers are needed
       on the day shift
    C. the City needs about as many civil service workers
       as there are people in Syracuse
    D. the services of some people who live in Syracuse
       is required

24. According to the above paragraph, it is MOST reasonable   24._____
    to assume that in New York City's civil service
    A. a worker can do any job that needs doing
    B. each worker works at a different job
    C. some workers work at more than one job
    D. some workers work at the same jobs

QUESTIONS 25-28.
Answer questions 25 to 28 *ONLY* on the basis of the information
given in the following paragraph.

The National and City flags are displayed daily from those public
buildings which are equipped with vertical or horizontal flag staffs.
Where a building has only one flag staff, only the National flag is
displayed. When the National flag is to be raised at the same time
as other flags, the National flag shall be raised about 6 feet in
advance of the other flags; if the flags are raised separately, the
National flag shall always be raised first. When more than one flag
is flown on horizontal staffs, the National flag shall be flown so
that it is to the extreme left as the observer faces the flag.
When more than one flag is displayed, they should all by the same
size. Under no circumstances should the National flag be smaller
in size than any other flag in a combination display. The standard
size for flags flown from City buildings is 5' x 8'.

25. From the above paragraph, a REASONABLE conclusion about   25.____
    flag staffs on public buildings is that a public building
      A. might have no flag staff at all
      B. needs two flag staffs
      C. should have at least one flag staff
      D. usually has a horizontal and a vertical flag staff

26. According to the above paragraph, a public building that   26.____
    has only one flag staff should raise the National flag
      A. and no other flag
      B. at sunrise
      C. first and then the City flag
      D. six feet in advance of any other flag

27. According to the above paragraph, the order, from left   27.____
    to right, in which the National flag flying from one of
    four horizontal staffs appear to a person who is facing
    the flag staffs is:
      A. Flag 1, flag 2, flag 3, National flag
      B. National flag, flag 1, flag 2, flag 3
      C. Flag 1, flag 2, National flag, flag 3
      D. Flag 1, National flag, flag 2, flag 3

28. According to the above paragraph, a combination display   28.____
    of flags on a City building would *usually* have
      A. a 6' x 10' National flag
      B. all flags 5' x 8' size
      C. all other flags smaller than the National flag
      D. 5' x 8' National and City flags and smaller sized
         other flags

QUESTIONS 29-30.
Answer questions 29 to 30 *ONLY* on the basis of the information
given in the following paragraph.

 Supplies are to be ordered from the stock room once a week. The
standard requisition form, Form SP 21, is to be used for ordering
all supplies. The form is prepared in triplicate, one white
original and two green copies. The white and one green copy are
sent to the stock room, and the remaining green copy is to be kept
by the orderer until the supplies are received.

29. According to the above paragraph, there is a limit on the 29.____
      A. amount of supplies that may be ordered
      B. day on which supplies may be ordered
      C. different kinds of supplies that may be ordered
      D. number of times supplies may be ordered in one year

30. According to the above paragraph, when the standard   30.____
    requisition form for supplies is prepared
      A. a total of four requisition blanks is used
      B. a white form is the original
      C. each copy is printed in two colors
      D. one copy is kept by the stock clerk

QUESTIONS 31-55.
Each of questions 31 to 55 consists of a word in capital letters
followed by four suggested meanings of the word. For each question,
choose the word or phrase which means *most nearly* the SAME as the
word in capital letters.

31. ABOLISH   31.____
    A. count up   B. do away with
    C. give more   D. pay double for

32. ABUSE   32.____
    A. accept   B. mistreat
    C. respect   D. touch

33. ACCURATE   33.____
    A. correct   B. lost
    C. neat   D. secret

34. ASSISTANCE   34.____
    A. attendance   B. belief
    C. help   D. reward

35. CAUTIOUS   35.____
    A. brave   B. careful
    C. greedy   D. hopeful

36. COURTEOUS   36.____
    A. better   B. easy
    C. polite   D. religious

37. CRITICIZE   37.____
    A. admit   B. blame
    C. check on   D. make dirty

38. DIFFICULT   38.____
    A. capable   B. dangerous
    C. dull   D. hard

39. ENCOURAGE   39.____
    A. aim at   B. beg for
    C. cheer on   D. free from

40. EXTENT   40.____
    A. age   B. size
    C. truth   D. wildness

41. EXTRAVAGANT   41.____
    A. empty   B. helpful
    C. over   D. wasteful

42. FALSE   42.____
    A. absent   B. colored
    C. not enough   D. wrong

43. INDICATE   43.____
    A. point out   B. show up
    C. shrink from   D. take to

44. NEGLECT   44.____
    A. disregard   B. flatten
    C. likeness   D. thoughtfulness

45. PENALIZE   45.____
    A. make   B. notice
    C. pay   D. punish

46. POSTPONED   46.____
    A. put off   B. repeated
    C. taught   D. went to

47. PUNCTUAL   47.____
    A. bursting   B. catching
    C. make a hole in   D. on time

48. RARE   48.____
    A. large   B. ride up
    C. unusual   D. young

49. RELY   49.____
    A. depend   B. do again
    C. use   D. wait for

50. REVEAL   50.____
    A. leave   B. renew
    C. soften   D. tell

51. SERIOUS   51.____
    A. important   B. order
    C. sharp   D. tight

52. TRIVIAL   52.____
    A. alive   B. empty
    C. petty   D. troublesome

53. VENTILATE   53.____
    A. air out   B. darken
    C. last   D. take a chance

54. VOLUNTARY   54.____
    A. common   B. paid
    C. sharing   D. willing

55. WHOLESOME   55.____
    A. cheap   B. healthful
    C. hot   D. together

56. An employee earns $48 a day and works 5 days a week.   56.____
    He will earn $2,160 in _____ weeks.
    A. 5   B. 7   C. 8   D. 9

57. In a certain bureau the entire staff consists of 1   57.____
    senior supervisor, 2 supervisors, 6 assistant super-
    visors and 54 associate workers. The per cent of the
    staff who are NOT associate workers is *most nearly*
    A. 14   B. 21   C. 27   D. 32

58. In a certain bureau, five employees each earn $1,000 a   58.____
    month, another three employees each earn $1,200 a month
    and another two employees each earn $4,100 a month.
    The monthly payroll for those employees is
    A. 3,600   B. 8,800   C. 11,400   D. 12,000

59. An employee contributes 5% of his salary to the pension   59.____
    fund. If his salary is $1,200 a month, the amount of his
    contribution to the pension fund in a year is
    A. 480   B. 720   C. 960   D. 1,200

60. The amount of square feet in an area that is 50 feet   60.____
    long and 30 feet wide is
    A. 80   B. 150   C. 800   D. 1,500

61. An injured person who is unconscious should NOT be   61.____
    given a liquid to drink *mainly* because
    A. cold liquid may be harmful
    B. he may choke on it
    C. he may not like the liquid
    D. his unconsciousness may be due to too much liquid

62. The MOST important reason for putting a bandage on a   62.____
    cut is to
    A. help prevent germs from getting into the cut
    B. hide the ugly scar
    C. keep the blood pressure down
    D. keep the skin warm

63. In first aid for an injured person, the MAIN purpose   63.____
    of a tourniquet is to
    A. prevent infection
    B. restore circulation
    C. support a broken bone
    D. stop severe bleeding

64. Artificial respiration is given in first aid *mainly* to   64.____
    A. force air into the lungs
    B. force blood circulation by even pressure
    C. keep the injured person awake
    D. prevent shock by keeping the victim's body in motion

65. The aromatic spirits of ammonia in a first aid kit should 65.____
    be used to
    A. clean a dirty wound
    B. deaden pain

    C. revive a person who has fainted
    D. warm a person who is chilled

QUESTIONS 66-70.
Read the chart below showing the absences in Unit A for the period November 1 through November 15; then answer questions 66 to 70 according to the information given.

ABSENCE RECORD - UNIT A

November 1 - 15

Date:	1	2	3	4	5	6	7	8	9	10	11	12	13	14	15
Employee															
Ames	X	S	H				X			H				X	X
Bloom	X		H			X	X	S	S	H	S	S			X
Deegan	X	J	H	J	J	J	X	X		H					X
Howard	X		H				X			H				X	X
Jergens	X	M	H	M	M	M	X			H				X	X
Lange	X		H			S	X	X							X
Morton	X						X	X	V	V	H				X
O'Shea	X		H			O	X			H	X			X	X

Code for Types of Absence

    X - Saturday or Sunday
    H - Legal Holiday
    P - Leave without pay
    M - Military leave
    J - Jury duty
    V - Vacation
    S - Sick leave
    O - Other leave or absence

   Note: If there is no entry against an employee's name under
         a date, the employee worked on that date.

66. According to the above chart, NO employee in Unit A was   66.____
    absent on
        A. leave without pay
        B. military leave
        C. other leave of absence
        D. vacation

67. According to the above chart, all but one of the employ-   67.____
    ees in Unit A were present on the
        A. 3rd   B. 5th   C. 9th   D. 13th

68. According to the above chart, the *only* employees who   68.____
    worked on a legal holiday when the other employees were
    absent are
        A. Deegan and Morton   B. Howard and O'Shea
        C. Lange and Morton   D. Morton and O'Shea

69. According to the above chart, the employee who was   69.____
    absent *only* on a day that was either a Saturday, Sunday
    or legal holiday was
        A. Bloom   B. Howard   C. Morton   D. O'Shea

70. The employee who had more absences than anyone else are   70._____
    A. Bloom and Deegan
    B. Bloom, Deegan, and Jergens
    C. Deegan and Jergens
    D. Deegan, Jergens, and O'Shea

KEY (CORRECT ANSWERS)

1. B	16. C	31. B	46. A	61. B
2. B	17. B	32. B	47. D	62. A
3. C	18. C	33. A	48. C	63. D
4. C	19. D	34. C	49. A	64. A
5. A	20. D	35. B	50. D	65. C
6. B	21. B	36. C	51. A	66. A
7. D	22. D	37. B	52. C	67. D
8. A	23. C	38. D	53. A	68. A
9. C	24. D	39. C	54. D	69. B
10. C	25. A	40. B	55. B	70. B
11. D	26. A	41. D	56. D	
12. B	27. B	42. D	57. A	
13. A	28. B	43. A	58. C	
14. C	29. D	44. A	59. B	
15. B	30. B	45. D	60. D	

TEST 2

DIRECTIONS: Each question consists of a statement. You are to
indicate whether the statement is TRUE (T) or FALSE (F).
*PRINT THE LETTER OF THE CORRECT ANSWER IN THE SPACE AT
THE RIGHT.*

QUESTIONS 1-4.
Read the paragraph below about "shock" and then answer questions
1 to 4 according to the information given in the paragraph.

SHOCK

While not found in all injuries, shock is present in all
serious injuries caused by accidents. During shock, the normal
activities of the body slow down. This partly explains why one
of the signs of shock is a pale, cold skin, since insufficient
blood goes to the body parts during shock.

1. If the injury caused by an accident is serious, shock is   1._____
   sure to be present.

2. In shock, the heart beats faster than normal.   2._____

3. The face of a person suffering from shock is usually red   3._____
   and flushed.

4. Not enough blood goes to different parts of the body   4._____
   during shock.

QUESTIONS 5-8.
Read the paragraph below about carbon monoxide gas and then
answer questions 5 to 8 according to the information given in
this paragraph.

CARBON MONOXIDE GAS

Carbon monoxide is a deadly gas from the effects of which
no one is immune. Any person's strength will be cut down considerably by breathing this gas, even though he does not take in
enough to overcome him. Wearing a handkerchief tied around the
nose and mouth offers some protection against the irritating fumes
of ordinary smoke, but many people have died convinced that a
handkerchief will stop carbon monoxide. Any person entering a
room filled with this deadly gas should wear a mask equipped with
an air hose, or even better, an oxygen breathing apparatus.

5. Some people get no ill effects from carbon monoxide gas   5._____
   until they are overcome.

6. A person can die from breathing carbon monoxide gas.   6._____

7. A handkerchief around the mouth and nose gives some pro-   7._____
   tection against the effects of ordinary smoke.

8. It is better for a person entering a room filled with   8.____
   carbon monixide to wear a mask equipped with an air hose
   than an oxygen breathing apparatus.

QUESTIONS 9-17.
Read the paragraph below about moving an office and then answer
questions 9 to 17 according to the information given in the
paragraph.

MOVING AN OFFICE

     An office with all its equipment is sometimes moved during
working hours. This is a difficult task, and must be done in an
orderly manner to avoid confusion. The operation should be planned
in such a way as not to interrupt the progress of work usually done
in the office and to make possible the accurate placement of the
furniture and records in the new location. If the office moves to
a place inside the same building, the desks and files are moved
with all their contents. If the movement is to another building,
the contents of each desk and file are placed in boxes. Each box
is marked with a letter showing the particular section in the new
quarters to which it is to be moved. Also marked on each box is the
number of the desk or file on which the box is to be placed. Each
piece of equipment must have a numbered tag. The number of each
piece of equipment is put in soft chalk on the floor in the new
office to show the proper location, and several floor plans are
made to show where each piece of equipment goes. When the moving
is done someone is stationed at each of the several exits of the
old office to see that each box or piece of equipment has its
destination clearly marked on it. At the new office someone stands
at each of the several entrances with a copy of the floor plan, and
directs the placing of the furniture and equipment according to the
floor plan. No one should interfere at this point with the arrangements shown on the plan. Improvements in arrangement can be considered and made at a later date.

9. It is a hard job to move an office from one place to   9.____
   another during working hours.

10. Confusion CANNOT be avoided if an office is moved during 10.____
    working hours.

11. The work usually done in an office must be stopped for   11.____
    the day when the office is moved during working hours.

12. If an office is moved from one floor to another in the   12.____
    same building, the contents of a desk are taken out and
    put into boxes for moving.

13. If boxes are used to hold material from desks when moving 13.____
    an office, the box is numbered the same as the desk on
    which it is to be put.

14. Letters are marked in soft chalk on the floor at new   14.____
    quarters to show where the desks should go when moved.

15. When the moving begins, a person is put at each exit of   15.____
    the old office to check that each box and piece of
    equipment has clearly marked on it where it is to go.

16. A person stationed at each entrance of the new quarters   16.____
    to direct the placing of the furniture and equipment has
    a copy of the floor plan of the new quarters.

17. If, while the furniture is being moved into the new   17.____
    office, a person helping at a doorway gets an idea of
    a better way to arrange the furniture, he should change
    the planned arrangement and make a record of the change.

QUESTIONS 18-25.
Read the paragraph below about polishing brass fixtures and then
answer questions 18 to 25 according to the information given in
this paragraph.

POLISHING BRASS FIXTURES

    Uncoated brass should be polished in the usual way using
brass polish. Special attention need be given only to brass
fixtures coated with lacquer. The surface of these fixtures will
not endure abrasive cleaners or polishes and should be cleaned
regularly with mild soap and water. Lacquer seldom fails to properly protect the surface of brass for the period guaranteed by the
manufacturer. But, if the attendant finds darkening or corrosion,
or any other symptom of failure of the lacquer, he should notify
his foreman. If the guarantee period has not expired, the foreman
will have the article returned to the manufacturer. If the guarantee period is over, it is necessary to first remove the old
lacquer, refinish and then relacquer the fixture at the agency's
shop. It is emphasized that all brass polish contains some
abrasive. For this reason, no brass polish should be used on
lacquered brass.

18. All brass fixtures should be cleaned in a special way.   18.____

19. A mild brass polish is good for cleaning brass fixtures
    coated with clear lacquer.

20. Lacquer coating on brass fixtures usually protects the   20.____
    surfaces for the period of the manufacturer's guarantee.

21. If an attendant finds corrosion in any lacquered brass   21.____
    article, he should relacquer the article.

22. The attendant should notify his foreman of failure of   22.____
    lacquer on a brass fixture only if the period of guarantee
    has expired.

23. The brass fixtures relacquered at the agency's shops are   23.____
    those on which the manufacturer's guarantee has expired.

24. Before a brass fixture is relacquered, the old lacquer   24.____
should be taken off.

25. Brass polish should NOT be used on lacquered surfaces   25.____
because it contains acid.

QUESTIONS 26-50.
Questions 26 to 50 relate to word meaning.

26. "The foreman had received a few requests." In this   26.____
sentence, the word 'requests' means *nearly* the SAME as
'complaints.'

27. "The procedure for doing the work was modified." In   27.____
this sentence, the word 'modified' means *nearly* the
SAME as 'discovered.'

28. "He stressed the importance of doing the job right."   28.____
In this sentence, the word 'stressed' means *nearly* the
SAME as 'discovered.'

29. "He worked with rapid movements." In this sentence, the 29.____
word 'rapid' means *nearly* the SAME as 'slow.'

30. "The man resumed his work when the foreman came in." In 30.____
this sentence, the word 'resumed' means *nearly* the SAME
as 'stopped.'

31. "The interior door would not open." In this sentence,   31.____
the word 'interior' means *nearly* the SAME as 'inside.'

32. "He extended his arm." In this sentence, the word   32.____
'extended' means *nearly* the SAME as 'stretched out.'

33. "He answered promptly." In this sentence, the word   33.____
'promptly' means *nearly* the SAME as 'quickly.'

34. "He punctured a piece of rubber." In this sentence,   34.____
the word 'punctured' means *nearly* the SAME as 'bought.'

35. "A few men were assisting the attendant." In this   35.____
sentence, the word 'assisting' means *nearly* the SAME
as 'helping.'

36. "He opposed the idea of using a vacuum cleaner for this 36.____
job." In this sentence, the word 'opposed' means *nearly*
the SAME as 'suggested.'

37. "Four employees were selected." In this sentence, the   37.____
word 'selected' means *nearly* the SAME as 'chosen.'

38. "This man is constantly supervised." In this sentence, 38.____
the word 'constantly' means *nearly* the SAME as 'rarely.'

39. "One part of soap to two parts of water is sufficient." In this sentence, the word 'sufficient' means *nearly* the SAME as 'enough.'   39.____

40. "The fire protection system was inadequate." In this sentence, the word 'inadequate' means *nearly* the SAME as 'enough.'   40.____

41. "The nozzle of the hose was clogged." In this sentence, the word 'clogged' means *nearly* the SAME as 'brass.'   41.____

42. "He resembles the man who worked here before." In this sentence, the word 'resembles,' means *nearly* the SAME as 'replaces.'   42.____

43. "They eliminated a number of items." In this sentence, the word 'eliminated' means *nearly* the SAME as 'bought.'   43.____

44. "He is a dependable worker." In this sentence, the word 'dependable' means *nearly* the SAME as 'poor.'   44.____

45. "Some wood finishes color the wood and conceal the natural grain." In this sentence, the word 'conceal' means *nearly* the SAME as 'hide.'   45.____

46. "Paint that is chalking sometimes retains its protective value." In this sentence, the word 'retains' means *nearly* the SAME as 'keeps.'   46.____

47. "Wood and trash had accumulated." In this sentence, the word 'accumulated' means *nearly* the SAME as 'piled up.'   47.____

48. An 'inflammable' liquid is one that is easily set on fire.   48.____

49. "The amounts were then compared." In this sentence, the word 'compared' means *nearly* the SAME as 'added.'   49.____

50. "The boy had fallen into a shallow pool." In this sentence, the work 'shallow' means *nearly* the SAME as 'deep.'   50.____

KEY (CORRECT ANSWERS)

1. T	11. F	21. F	31. T	41. F
2. F	12. F	22. F	32. T	42. F
3. F	13. T	23. T	33. T	43. F
4. T	14. F	24. T	34. F	44. F
5. F	15. T	25. F	35. T	45. T
6. T	16. T	26. F	36. F	46. T
7. T	17. F	27. T	37. T	47. T
8. F	18. F	28. F	38. F	48. T
9. T	19. F	29. F	39. T	49. F
10. F	20. T	30. F	40. F	50. F

ARITHMETIC

EXAMINATION SECTION

DIRECTIONS FOR THIS SECTION:
Each question or incomplete statement is followed by several suggested answers or completions. Select the one that *BEST* answers the question or completes the statement. *PRINT THE LETTER OF THE CORRECT ANSWER IN THE SPACE AT THE RIGHT.*

TEST 1

1. Add $4.34, $34.50, $6.00, $101.76, $90.67. From the result, subtract $60.54 and $10.56.
   A. $76.17   B. $156.37   C. $166.17   D. $300.37   1. ...

2. Add 2,200, 2,600, 252 and 47.96. From the result, subtract 202.70, 1,200, 2,150 and 434.43.
   A. 1,112.83   B. 1,213.46   C. 1,341.51   D. 1,348.91   2. ...

3. Multiply 1850 by .05 and multiply 3300 by .08 and, then, add both results.
   A. 242.50   B. 264.00   C. 333.25   D. 356.50   3. ...

4. Multiply 312.77 by .04. Round off the result to the nearest hundredth.
   A. 12.52   B. 12.511   C. 12.518   D. 12.51   4. ...

5. Add 362.05, 91.13, 347.81 and 17.46 and then divide the result by 6. The answer, rounded off to the nearest hundredth, is:
   A. 138.409   B. 137.409   C. 136.41   D. 136.40   5. ...

6. Add 66.25 and 15.06 and, then, multiply the result by 2 1/6. The answer is, most nearly,
   A. 176.18   B. 176.17   C. 162.66   D. 162.62   6. ...

7. Each of the following items contains three decimals. In which case do *all* three decimals have the *SAME* value?
   A. .3; .30; .03   B. .25; .250; .2500
   C. 1.9; 1.90; 1.09   D. .35; .350; .035   7. ...

8. Add 1/2 the sum of (539.84 and 479.26) to 1/3 the sum of (1461.93 and 927.27). Round off the result to the nearest whole number.
   A. 3408   B. 2899   C. 1816   D. 1306   8. ...

9. Multiply $5,906.09 by 15% and, then, divide the result by 1/3.
   A. $295.30   B. $885.91   C. $8,859.14   D. $29,530.45   9. ...

10. Multiply 630 by 517.
    A. 325,710   B. 345,720   C. 362,425   D. 385,660   10. ...

11. Multiply 35 by 846.
    A. 4050   B. 9450   C. 18740   D. 29610   11. ...

12. Multiply 823 by 0.05.
    A. 0.4115   B. 4.115   C. 41.15   D. 411.50   12. ...

13. Multiply 1690 by 0.10.
    A. 0.169   B. 1.69   C. 16.90   D. 169.0   13. ...

14. Divide 2765 by 35.
    A. 71   B. 79   C. 87   D. 93   14. ...

15. From $18.55 subtract $6.80.
    A. $9.75   B. $10.95   C. $11.75   D. $25.35   15. ...

16. The sum of 2.75 + 4.50 + 3.60 is:
    A. 9.75   B. 10.85   C. 11.15   D. 11.95   16. ...

17. The sum of 9.63 + 11.21 + 17.25 is:
    A. 36.09   B. 38.09   C. 39.92   D. 41.22   17. ...

18. The sum of 112.0 + 16.9 + 3.84 is:
    A. 129.3   B. 132.74   C. 136.48   D. 167.3   18. ...

19. When 65 is added to the result of 14 multiplied by 13, the   19. ...
    answer is:
    A. 92   B. 182   C. 247   D. 16055
20. From $391.55 subtract $273.45.   20. ...
    A. $118.10   B. $128.20   C. $178.10   D. $218.20

———

TEST 2

1. The sum of $29.61 + $101.53 + $943.64 is: 1. ...
   A. $983.88   B. $1074.78   C. $1174.98   D. $1341.42
2. The sum of $132.25 + $85.63 + $7056.44 is: 2. ...
   A. $1694.19   B. $7274.32   C. $8464.57   D. $9346.22
3. The sum of 4010 + 1271 + 838 + 23 is: 3. ...
   A. 6142   B. 6162   C. 6242   D. 6362
4. The sum of 53632 + 27403 + 98765 + 75424 is: 4. ...
   A. 19214   B. 215214   C. 235224   D. 255224
5. The sum of 76342 + 49050 + 21206 + 59989 is: 5. ...
   A. 196586   B. 206087   C. 206587   D. 234487
6. The sum of $452.13 + $963.45 + $621.25 is: 6. ...
   A. $1936.83   B. $2036.83   C. $2095.73   D. $2135.73
7. The sum of 36392 + 42156 + 98765 is: 7. ...
   A. 167214   B. 177203   C. 177313   D. 178213
8. The sum of 40125 + 87123 + 24689 is: 8. ...
   A. 141827   B. 151827   C. 151937   D. 161947
9. The sum of 2379 + 4015 + 6521 + 9986 is: 9. ...
   A. 22901   B. 22819   C. 21801   D. 21791
10. From 50962 subtract 36197.   10. ...
    A. 14675   B. 14765   C. 14865   D. 24765
11. From 90000 subtract 31928.   11. ...
    A. 58072   B. 59062   C. 68172   D. 69182
12. From 63764 subtract 21548.   12. ...
    A. 42216   B. 43122   C. 45126   D. 85312
13. From $9605.13 subtract $2715.96.   13. ...
    A. $12,321.09 B. $8,690.16   C. $6,990.07   D. $6,889.17
14. From 76421 subtract 73101.   14. ...
    A. 3642   B. 3540   C. 3320   D. 3242
15. From $8.25 subtract $6.50.   15. ...
    A. $1.25   B. $1.50   C. $1.75   D. $2.25
16. Multiply 583 by 0.50.   16. ...
    A. $291.50   B. 28.15   C. 2.815   D. 0.2815
17. Multiply 0.35 by 1045.   17. ...
    A. 0.36575   B. 3.6575   C. 36.575   D. 365.75
18. Multiply 25 by 2513.   18. ...
    A. 62825   B. 62725   C. 60825   D. 52825
19. Multiply 423 by 0.01.   19. ...
    A. 0.0423   B. 0.423   C. 4.23   D. 42.3
20. Multiply 6.70 by 3.2.   20. ...
    A. 2.1440   B. 21.440   C. 214.40   D. 2144.0

———

TEST 3

Questions 1-4.
DIRECTIONS: For each of Questions 1-4, perform the indicated arithmetic and choose the correct answer from among the four choices given.

1. 12,485
   +   347
   A. 12,038   B. 12,128   C. 12,782   D. 12,832   1. ...

2. 74,137
   +   711
   A. 74,326   B. 74,848   C. 78,028   D. 78,926   2. ...

3. 3,749
   - 671
   A. 3,078   B. 3,168   C. 4,028   D. 4,420   3. ...

4. 19,805
   -18,904
   A. 109   B. 901   C. 1,109   D. 1,901   4. ...

5. When 119 is subtracted from the sum of 2016 + 1634, the   5. ...
   remainder is:
   A. 2460   B. 3531   C. 3650   D. 3769

6. Multiply 35 X 65 X 15.   6. ...
   A. 2275   B. 24265   C. 31145   D. 34125

7. 90% expressed as a decimal is: 7. ...
   A. .009   B. .09   C. .9   D. 9.0

8. Seven-tenths of a foot expressed in inches is: 8. ...
   A. 5.5   B. 6.5   C. 7   D. 8.4

9. If 95 men were divided into crews of five men each, the   9. ...
   number of crews that will be formed is:
   A. 16   B. 17   C. 18   D. 19

10. If a man earns $19.50 a day, the *number* of working days   10. ...
    it will take him to earn $4,875 is, most nearly,
    A. 225   B. 250   C. 275   D. 300

11. If 5½ loads of gravel cost $55.00, then 6½ loads will   11. ...
    cost:
    A. $60.   B. $62.50   C. $65.   D. $66.00

12. At $2.50 a yard, 27 yards of concrete will cost: 12. ...
    A. $36.   B. $41.80   C. $54.   D. $67.50

13. A distance is measured and found to be 52.23 feet. In   13. ...
    feet and inches, this distance is, most nearly, 52 feet
    and
    A. 2 3/4"   B. 3 1/4"   C. 3 3/4"   D. 4 1/4"

14. If a maintainer gets $5.20 per hour and time and one-half   14. ...
    for working over 40 hours, his *gross* salary for a week in
    which he worked 43 hours would be
    A. $208.00   B. $223.60   C. $231.40   D. $335.40

15. The circumference of a circle is given by the formula   15. ...
    C = ∏D, where C is the circumference, D is the diameter,
    and ∏ is about 3 1/7.
    If a coil is 15 turns of steel cable has an average diameter
    of 20 inches, the *total* length of cable on the coil is
    nearest to
    A. 5 feet   B. 78 feet   C. 550 feet   D. 943 feet

16. The measurements of a poured concrete foundation show   16. ...
    that 54 cubic feet of concrete have been placed.
    If payment for this concrete is to be on the basis of
    cubic yards, the 54 cubic feet must be
    A. multiplied by 27   B. multiplied by 3
    C. divided by 27   D. divided by 3

17. If the cost of 4 1/2 tons of structural steel is $1,800,   17. ...
    then the cost of 12 tons is, most nearly,
       A. $4,800   B. $5,400   C. $7,200   D. $216,000
18. An hourly-paid employee working 12:00 midnight to 8:00   18. ...
    a.m. is directed to report to the medical staff for a
    physical examination at 11:00 a.m. of the same day.
    The pay allowed him for reporting will be
       A. 1 hour   B. 2 hours   C. 3 hours   D. 4 hours
19. The *total* length of four pieces of 2" pipe, whose lengths   19. ...
    are 7' 3½", 4' 2 3/16", 5' 7 5/16", and 8' 5 7/8", re-
    spectively, is:
       A. 24' 6 3/4"   B. 24' 7 15/16"
       C. 25' 5 13/16"   D. 25' 6 7/8"
20. As a senior mortuary caretaker, you are preparing a month-   20. ...
    ly report, using the following figures:
       No. of bodies received   983
       No. of bodies claimed   720
       No. of bodies sent to city cemetery   14
       No. of bodies sent to medical schools   9
    How many bodies remained at the end of the monthly report-
    ing period?
       A. 230   B. 240   C. 250   D. 260

———

KEYS (CORRECT ANSWERS)

TEST 1		TEST 2		TEST 3	
1. C	11. D	1. B	11. A	1. D	11. C
2. A	12. C	2. B	12. A	2. B	12. D
3. D	13. D	3. A	13. D	3. A	13. A
4. D	14. B	4. D	14. C	4. B	14. C
5. C	15. C	5. C	15. C	5. B	15. B
6. B	16. B	6. B	16. A	6. D	16. C
7. B	17. B	7. C	17. D	7. C	17. A
8. D	18. B	8. C	18. A	8. D	18. C
9. A	19. C	9. A	19. C	9. D	19. D
10. A	20. A	10. B	20. B	10. B	20. B

———

ANSWER SHEET

USE THE SPECIAL PENCIL.   MAKE GLOSSY BLACK MARKS.

	A B C D E		A B C D E		A B C D E		A B C D E		A B C D E
1	⋮⋮⋮⋮⋮	26	⋮⋮⋮⋮⋮	51	⋮⋮⋮⋮⋮	76	⋮⋮⋮⋮⋮	101	⋮⋮⋮⋮⋮
2	⋮⋮⋮⋮⋮	27	⋮⋮⋮⋮⋮	52	⋮⋮⋮⋮⋮	77	⋮⋮⋮⋮⋮	102	⋮⋮⋮⋮⋮
3	⋮⋮⋮⋮⋮	28	⋮⋮⋮⋮⋮	53	⋮⋮⋮⋮⋮	78	⋮⋮⋮⋮⋮	103	⋮⋮⋮⋮⋮
4	⋮⋮⋮⋮⋮	29	⋮⋮⋮⋮⋮	54	⋮⋮⋮⋮⋮	79	⋮⋮⋮⋮⋮	104	⋮⋮⋮⋮⋮
5	⋮⋮⋮⋮⋮	30	⋮⋮⋮⋮⋮	55	⋮⋮⋮⋮⋮	80	⋮⋮⋮⋮⋮	105	⋮⋮⋮⋮⋮
6	⋮⋮⋮⋮⋮	31	⋮⋮⋮⋮⋮	56	⋮⋮⋮⋮⋮	81	⋮⋮⋮⋮⋮	106	⋮⋮⋮⋮⋮
7	⋮⋮⋮⋮⋮	32	⋮⋮⋮⋮⋮	57	⋮⋮⋮⋮⋮	82	⋮⋮⋮⋮⋮	107	⋮⋮⋮⋮⋮
8	⋮⋮⋮⋮⋮	33	⋮⋮⋮⋮⋮	58	⋮⋮⋮⋮⋮	83	⋮⋮⋮⋮⋮	108	⋮⋮⋮⋮⋮
9	⋮⋮⋮⋮⋮	34	⋮⋮⋮⋮⋮	59	⋮⋮⋮⋮⋮	84	⋮⋮⋮⋮⋮	109	⋮⋮⋮⋮⋮
10	⋮⋮⋮⋮⋮	35	⋮⋮⋮⋮⋮	60	⋮⋮⋮⋮⋮	85	⋮⋮⋮⋮⋮	110	⋮⋮⋮⋮⋮

Make only ONE mark for each answer.   Additional and stray marks may be
counted as mistakes.   In making corrections, erase errors COMPLETELY.

	A B C D E		A B C D E		A B C D E		A B C D E		A B C D E
11	⋮⋮⋮⋮⋮	36	⋮⋮⋮⋮⋮	61	⋮⋮⋮⋮⋮	86	⋮⋮⋮⋮⋮	111	⋮⋮⋮⋮⋮
12	⋮⋮⋮⋮⋮	37	⋮⋮⋮⋮⋮	62	⋮⋮⋮⋮⋮	87	⋮⋮⋮⋮⋮	112	⋮⋮⋮⋮⋮
13	⋮⋮⋮⋮⋮	38	⋮⋮⋮⋮⋮	63	⋮⋮⋮⋮⋮	88	⋮⋮⋮⋮⋮	113	⋮⋮⋮⋮⋮
14	⋮⋮⋮⋮⋮	39	⋮⋮⋮⋮⋮	64	⋮⋮⋮⋮⋮	89	⋮⋮⋮⋮⋮	114	⋮⋮⋮⋮⋮
15	⋮⋮⋮⋮⋮	40	⋮⋮⋮⋮⋮	65	⋮⋮⋮⋮⋮	90	⋮⋮⋮⋮⋮	115	⋮⋮⋮⋮⋮
16	⋮⋮⋮⋮⋮	41	⋮⋮⋮⋮⋮	66	⋮⋮⋮⋮⋮	91	⋮⋮⋮⋮⋮	116	⋮⋮⋮⋮⋮
17	⋮⋮⋮⋮⋮	42	⋮⋮⋮⋮⋮	67	⋮⋮⋮⋮⋮	92	⋮⋮⋮⋮⋮	117	⋮⋮⋮⋮⋮
18	⋮⋮⋮⋮⋮	43	⋮⋮⋮⋮⋮	68	⋮⋮⋮⋮⋮	93	⋮⋮⋮⋮⋮	118	⋮⋮⋮⋮⋮
19	⋮⋮⋮⋮⋮	44	⋮⋮⋮⋮⋮	69	⋮⋮⋮⋮⋮	94	⋮⋮⋮⋮⋮	119	⋮⋮⋮⋮⋮
20	⋮⋮⋮⋮⋮	45	⋮⋮⋮⋮⋮	70	⋮⋮⋮⋮⋮	95	⋮⋮⋮⋮⋮	120	⋮⋮⋮⋮⋮
21	⋮⋮⋮⋮⋮	46	⋮⋮⋮⋮⋮	71	⋮⋮⋮⋮⋮	96	⋮⋮⋮⋮⋮	121	⋮⋮⋮⋮⋮
22	⋮⋮⋮⋮⋮	47	⋮⋮⋮⋮⋮	72	⋮⋮⋮⋮⋮	97	⋮⋮⋮⋮⋮	122	⋮⋮⋮⋮⋮
23	⋮⋮⋮⋮⋮	48	⋮⋮⋮⋮⋮	73	⋮⋮⋮⋮⋮	98	⋮⋮⋮⋮⋮	123	⋮⋮⋮⋮⋮
24	⋮⋮⋮⋮⋮	49	⋮⋮⋮⋮⋮	74	⋮⋮⋮⋮⋮	99	⋮⋮⋮⋮⋮	124	⋮⋮⋮⋮⋮
25	⋮⋮⋮⋮⋮	50	⋮⋮⋮⋮⋮	75	⋮⋮⋮⋮⋮	100	⋮⋮⋮⋮⋮	125	⋮⋮⋮⋮⋮

ANSWER SHEET

TEST NO. _____ PART _____ TITLE OF POSITION _____

PLACE OF EXAMINATION _____ DATE_____

(CITY OR TOWN)   (STATE)

RATING

USE THE SPECIAL PENCIL.   MAKE GLOSSY BLACK MARKS.

	A	B	C	D	E		A	B	C	D	E		A	B	C	D	E		A	B	C	D	E		A	B	C	D	E
1	::	::	::	::	::	26	::	::	::	::	::	51	::	::	::	::	::	76	::	::	::	::	::	101	::	::	::	::	::
2	::	::	::	::	::	27	::	::	::	::	::	52	::	::	::	::	::	77	::	::	::	::	::	102	::	::	::	::	::
3	::	::	::	::	::	28	::	::	::	::	::	53	::	::	::	::	::	78	::	::	::	::	::	103	::	::	::	::	::
4	::	::	::	::	::	29	::	::	::	::	::	54	::	::	::	::	::	79	::	::	::	::	::	104	::	::	::	::	::
5	::	::	::	::	::	30	::	::	::	::	::	55	::	::	::	::	::	80	::	::	::	::	::	105	::	::	::	::	::
6	::	::	::	::	::	31	::	::	::	::	::	56	::	::	::	::	::	81	::	::	::	::	::	106	::	::	::	::	::
7	::	::	::	::	::	32	::	::	::	::	::	57	::	::	::	::	::	82	::	::	::	::	::	107	::	::	::	::	::
8	::	::	::	::	::	33	::	::	::	::	::	58	::	::	::	::	::	83	::	::	::	::	::	108	::	::	::	::	::
9	::	::	::	::	::	34	::	::	::	::	::	59	::	::	::	::	::	84	::	::	::	::	::	109	::	::	::	::	::
10	::	::	::	::	::	35	::	::	::	::	::	60	::	::	::	::	::	85	::	::	::	::	::	110	::	::	::	::	::

Make only ONE mark for each answer.   Additional and stray marks may be counted as mistakes.   In making corrections, erase errors COMPLETELY.

	A	B	C	D	E		A	B	C	D	E		A	B	C	D	E		A	B	C	D	E		A	B	C	D	E
11	::	::	::	::	::	36	::	::	::	::	::	61	::	::	::	::	::	86	::	::	::	::	::	111	::	::	::	::	::
12	::	::	::	::	::	37	::	::	::	::	::	62	::	::	::	::	::	87	::	::	::	::	::	112	::	::	::	::	::
13	::	::	::	::	::	38	::	::	::	::	::	63	::	::	::	::	::	88	::	::	::	::	::	113	::	::	::	::	::
14	::	::	::	::	::	39	::	::	::	::	::	64	::	::	::	::	::	89	::	::	::	::	::	114	::	::	::	::	::
15	::	::	::	::	::	40	::	::	::	::	::	65	::	::	::	::	::	90	::	::	::	::	::	115	::	::	::	::	::
16	::	::	::	::	::	41	::	::	::	::	::	66	::	::	::	::	::	91	::	::	::	::	::	116	::	::	::	::	::
17	::	::	::	::	::	42	::	::	::	::	::	67	::	::	::	::	::	92	::	::	::	::	::	117	::	::	::	::	::
18	::	::	::	::	::	43	::	::	::	::	::	68	::	::	::	::	::	93	::	::	::	::	::	118	::	::	::	::	::
19	::	::	::	::	::	44	::	::	::	::	::	69	::	::	::	::	::	94	::	::	::	::	::	119	::	::	::	::	::
20	::	::	::	::	::	45	::	::	::	::	::	70	::	::	::	::	::	95	::	::	::	::	::	120	::	::	::	::	::
21	::	::	::	::	::	46	::	::	::	::	::	71	::	::	::	::	::	96	::	::	::	::	::	121	::	::	::	::	::
22	::	::	::	::	::	47	::	::	::	::	::	72	::	::	::	::	::	97	::	::	::	::	::	122	::	::	::	::	::
23	::	::	::	::	::	48	::	::	::	::	::	73	::	::	::	::	::	98	::	::	::	::	::	123	::	::	::	::	::
24	::	::	::	::	::	49	::	::	::	::	::	74	::	::	::	::	::	99	::	::	::	::	::	124	::	::	::	::	::
25	::	::	::	::	::	50	::	::	::	::	::	75	::	::	::	::	::	100	::	::	::	::	::	125	::	::	::	::	::